1·25

HAVE YOU FORGOTTEN YET?

Have you forgotten yet? . .
For the world's events have rumbled on since
those gagged days . . .
Siegfried Sassoon

HAVE YOU FORGOTTEN YET?

Between the Two World Wars

ALAN DELGADO

DAVID & CHARLES : NEWTON ABBOT

To Jane, Martin, Susan—
the captive audience

ISBN 0 7153 5807 3

Set in 11/12pt Imprint
and printed in Great Britain
by Biddles Limited Guildford
for David & Charles (Holdings) Limited
South Devon House Newton Abbot Devon

CONTENTS

AUTHOR'S NOTE

Describing events that have taken place during the formative years of a lifetime means that memory is sometimes relied upon to a greater extent than is safe for accuracy. The main historical events present few problems. It is in painting the backcloth against which the main scenes were enacted, that the colours may not always be true.

The period covered by this book is now 'history'. For some it was the 'good old days'; for others, with the class distinction, lack of opportunity and futile government, it was a time with few, if any, saving graces. But whatever one's views it is an important period from which stem many of our present-day ills, and some of our blessings.
        A.D.

THE SCENE-SHIFTERS

When I get my civvy clothes on
Oh, how happy I shall be.
When I get my civvy clothes on—
No more soldiering for me.
        Soldiers' song in 1914 War

IN LONDON the maroons firing at 11 am on 11 November 1918, heralded the Armistice. In the crowded streets, flags waved, whistles and bells sounded, strangers embraced, vehicles—commandeered and boarded—toured around in crazy fashion. The war was over. The slaughter, the hell of the trenches, the agonising anxiety, the need to obey and not to question, the monotony of bully beef and plum-and-apple jam, the boredom, the feverish activity, the mud, the ticks, the futility of it all—that was finished. It was possible to look forward to a better world in which nation would live in peace with nation; class barriers at home would be broken down; a man would return to his job and rebuild what had been so cruelly shattered. How often had the flagging spirits of those in the trenches been buoyed by a glance at a tattered snapshot of home and family? The only hope was for a 'blighty' to send one home, or for the luck to survive so that the dreams might come true.

But life was not going to be the same. The old job was not necessarily there, and even if it were, settling down to it might be difficult. The women, liberated from the formal Edwardian era, were no longer meek, defenceless creatures relying on male protection. The baby, left on joining up, was now a small boy; civilian life seemed dull to many returning soldiers; the easy comradeship of the war years was missing. At home, communication between man and wife had to begin again. Some returned to homes already broken by the strain of absence.

Disillusionment was not long in coming.

'What did you join the Army for?
Why did you join the Army?
What did you join the Army for? . . .

. . . You must have been bloodywell barmy'
Marching song, 1914–18 War

The Daily Chronicle

No. 17.702.   LONDON, TUESDAY, NOVEMBER 12, 1918.   ONE PENNY

END OF THE GREAT WORLD WAR.

Extra Late Edition.

SURRENDER OF GERMANY.

ARMISTICE SIGNED.

ALL FIGHTING SUBMARINES TO BE HANDED OVER.

The end of the world-wide war was announced yesterday in the House of Commons by the Prime Minister in the following historic declaration:—

The Armistice was signed at five o'clock this morning. Hostilities ceased on all fronts at 11 a.m. to-day. . . . Thus came to an end the cruellest and most terrible war that has ever scourged mankind. I hope we may say that thus, on this fateful morning, came to an end all wars.

CHIEF POINTS IN CONDITIONS OF ARMISTICE.

End of fighting by air, land and sea.

Evacuation of invaded lands—Belgium, France, Alsace-Lorraine, Luxemburg—and repatriation of all inhabitants of these lands, within 14 days.

Evacuation of countries on left

and all stocks, shares and money removed.

Restoration (to Allies in trust) of Russian or Rumanian gold yielded to, or taken by, Germany.

What Germany Surrenders.

Germany to surrender, in good condition:—

With you I rejoice and thank God for the victories which the Allied arms have won, bringing hostilities to an end and peace within sight.

[J. Russell & Sons.

[King George, from the balcony of Buckingham Palace.]

EX-KAISER A FUGITIVE.

UNCONFIRMED REPORT OF THE SHOOTING OF CROWN PRINCE.

PROBABLE INTERNMENT OF WILLIAM II.

HINDENBURG REMAINS AT GERMAN MAIN HEADQUARTERS.

William II. has fled to Holland, and as he crossed the frontier wearing a military uniform and sword, it is believed he will be interned.

Hindenburg, contrary to report, has not fled with his fallen master, but accompanying the party were the Kaiserin and at least one of her sons.

The following message was received at a late hour last night:—

AMSTERDAM, Monday.

It is reported that the Crown Prince has been shot. Details are lacking.—Central News.

HOW THE KAISER CAME.

CHANGES INTO CIVILIAN ATTIRE REACHING HOLLAND.

From "The Daily Chronicle" Special Correspondent, George Renwick.

AMSTERDAM, Monday.

It was on Sunday morning, almost precisely at 7.30, that the ex-Kaiser William II. saw the last of Germany and crossed the Belgian-Dutch frontier into exile.

On Saturday evening a German general arrived at Maastricht, and put himself into communication with the Dutch authorities, informing them that the ex-Kaiser would arrive on Dutch territory on the following day. At the hour I have mentioned a train of ten automobiles approached the little half Belgian half-Dutch village of Mossland, and drew up in the neighbourhood of the Customs Office.

upon another train. The two trains were sent under Dutch escort to Eysden, and kept there pending instructions from The Hague.

Here again the Kaiser appeared on the platform, this time in civilian clothes, and walked about for a little while. The larger number of the suite, however, kept out of sight.

It was in the train at the little station of Eysden that the ex-monarch spent the first night of exile. The station was held by soldiers and mounted police, and the public were kept at a good distance.

GEORGE RENWICK.

HINDENBURG REMAINS.

TO RECEIVE SOLDIERS' COUNCIL AT HEADQUARTERS.

AMSTERDAM, Monday.

A Berlin telegram denies that the

7

LLOYD GEORGE had headed a Coalition Government throughout the war. The post war electioneers promised a 'fit country for heroes to live in'—a phrase that was to become a hollow cliché. The election was coloured by the issues of revenge and compensation—'hang the Kaiser, make them pay'. The 'coupon' election, as it was called, took place on 14 December 1918, although votes were not counted until after Christmas, to allow time to include the soldiers' votes. The result was a clear victory for the Welsh Wizard and his Coalition Party, consisting mainly of Conservatives and Liberals. The Opposition comprised an impressive Labour return of fifty-nine members (the largest of the Opposition parties) a few Asquith Liberals, and a small number of Conservatives who would not toe the Coalition line. There was also a handful of Independents (including Irish Nationalists and Sinn Feiners who refused to take their seats).

Initially the demobilisation arrangements were not successful. The Ministry of Reconstruction had made plans some years before the war ended and their scheme was first to release the 'key' workers who could start up the wheels of industry; but this caused much bitter feeling as these workers' 'key' status had meant they had been the last to be conscripted. The Secretary of State for War, Winston Churchill, changed the priorities; it was to be first in, first out. Men left the forces at the rate of about 10,000 a day for almost six months.

Unemployment had been feared; but women were leaving the factories and returning to their homes. The business world, seeing a cheerful future, absorbed the thousands that wanted to get back to work. It was the officers who found it difficult to get employment. It seemed to be assumed that they had private means or were on the 'old boy' network. Many were in their mid-twenties or older, so what could they know of commerce? Integrity, leadership, ability to get on with one's fellows were admirable qualities, but as qualifications for a specific job they were of little use. These men had not the skills of workmen and could hardly join as office boys. Despairingly they went from interview to interview. Many sank their savings or any war gratuity into speculative business

(left) Jubilations; (right) decorations

Discord in Ireland. A prayer for peace in Downing Street. The year 1921

ventures; others rejoined the forces—in the ranks—and served in Germany with the Army of Occupation.

The winter of 1919 brought an influenza epidemic of such severity that in England and Wales some 150,000 died. The epidemic was not confined to Britain, the whole world was ravaged. The death toll amounted to some 27 million—twice the war casualties—although it was itself a result of the war. Coal was acutely scarce in Britain, nourishing foods were hard to come by, and five years of rationing had not improved stamina. The reaction after the elation of the Armistice had left people depressed, adjustments and uncertainty imposed

a strain, sapping ability to resist infection. All ages were affected; those who had survived the worst horrors of the battlefield succumbed to the raging epidemic.

A sickness began to pervade the business world too. Industrial unrest in 1919 heralded the beginning of the trouble in the first half of 1920. Wages failed to keep pace with the rapid increase in prices. By 1921 the downturn of the economy was being felt. The wild post-war spending-spree was halting; people had to watch the pence. Industry shed the load, and the load was human—the ex-serviceman.

The solution was seen, at the time, in cutting government expenditure. Sir Eric Geddes, the

9

one-time Minister of Transport, headed the committee which recommended specific economies. The 'Geddes Axe' made heavy cuts in the army, navy and air force; education, pensions, health and child-welfare services also suffered. The total cuts amounted to £64 million, against a recommended £75 million.

The Coalition Government was facing a crisis at home and abroad, problems that Lloyd George seemed unable to cope with effectively. Where was the land fit for heroes to live in? The promises made at the end of the war had not materialised. People were not better off and there was little sign of improvement. Even the peace was uneasy; nations were quarrelling and skirmishing. The Conservative Party seized this opportunity of regaining power under Bonar Law in October 1922. He resigned seven months later due to ill-health, and the premiership passed to Stanley Baldwin in May 1923.

Although the Great War had ended, conflicts between the nations continued, for a new balance had to be found. Some of the old established powers had been eclipsed; less important nations had gained in stature by being on the winning side, though their capacity for survival had been drained by the sacrifices they had been forced to make. The collapse of the Turkish empire presented the Allies with considerable problems, made worse by the general instability in eastern Europe. The Allies were forced to abandon their attempts to support the White Russians against the Bolsheviks, who overcame all resistance in Russia by July 1920.

Nearer home, Ireland was in torment. The Easter Rebellion of 1916 left bitter memories, and in 1920 the British still had at least 40,000 troops there; the IRA mustered some 15,000. Following the pattern of a force short in weapon power and manpower, but knowledgeable about the terrain, the IRA used ambushes, attacks on police stations and guerilla tactics against communications and individuals. The culmination was 'Bloody Sunday', 21 November 1920, when, among other violent incidents, British officers and civilians were dragged from their beds and shot.

'Partition' was not a new solution, it had been proposed during the earlier troubles, but a new Home Rule Bill in 1919 allowed two parliaments in Ireland—one in Dublin, and the other in Belfast. Ireland remained part of the United Kingdom but with wide powers of self-government (except over the levying of taxes). Nevertheless the strife continued with renewed intensity, and it was not until 1922 that a Free State Government was established, in which Northern Ireland wanted no part. The quarrels and the bloodshed temporarily subsided.

BY THE middle of the twenties, the British had come to accept the great changes brought about by the war. The leisurely Edwardian days would never return. The 'wrong' people now had money, and this resentment against the *nouveaux riches* and their ostentatious spending found its bitter expression in the image of the war profiteer, seen in cartoons as a bloated monster in a top hat with a cigar stuck aggressively in his mouth.

The social scene may have been less magnificent but it certainly survived. The glossy magazines—*The Bystander, Tatler, Sporting and Dramatic* mirrored the activities of the London 'season'. Being 'presented' to His Majesty was still essential to a debutante's 'coming out' and the cars choked the Mall on such occasions. The fashionable life of pleasure, Ascot, Henley, Cowes, Eton *v* Harrow at Lords, with Le Touquet, Cannes and Biarritz after the 'season' ended, was faithfully recorded in the smart weeklies. Earls, viscounts and barons were created by successive governments and those so elevated were eager to play their part in keeping the social scene revolving. Most of the new aristocrats were self-made men who had prospered during the war. They looked and behaved differently: and it showed.

Domestic help was still available. The daughters of the unemployed were happy to be placed in a good home where, although they might be overworked, they were not starved. A wage of £26 a year and 'all found' was

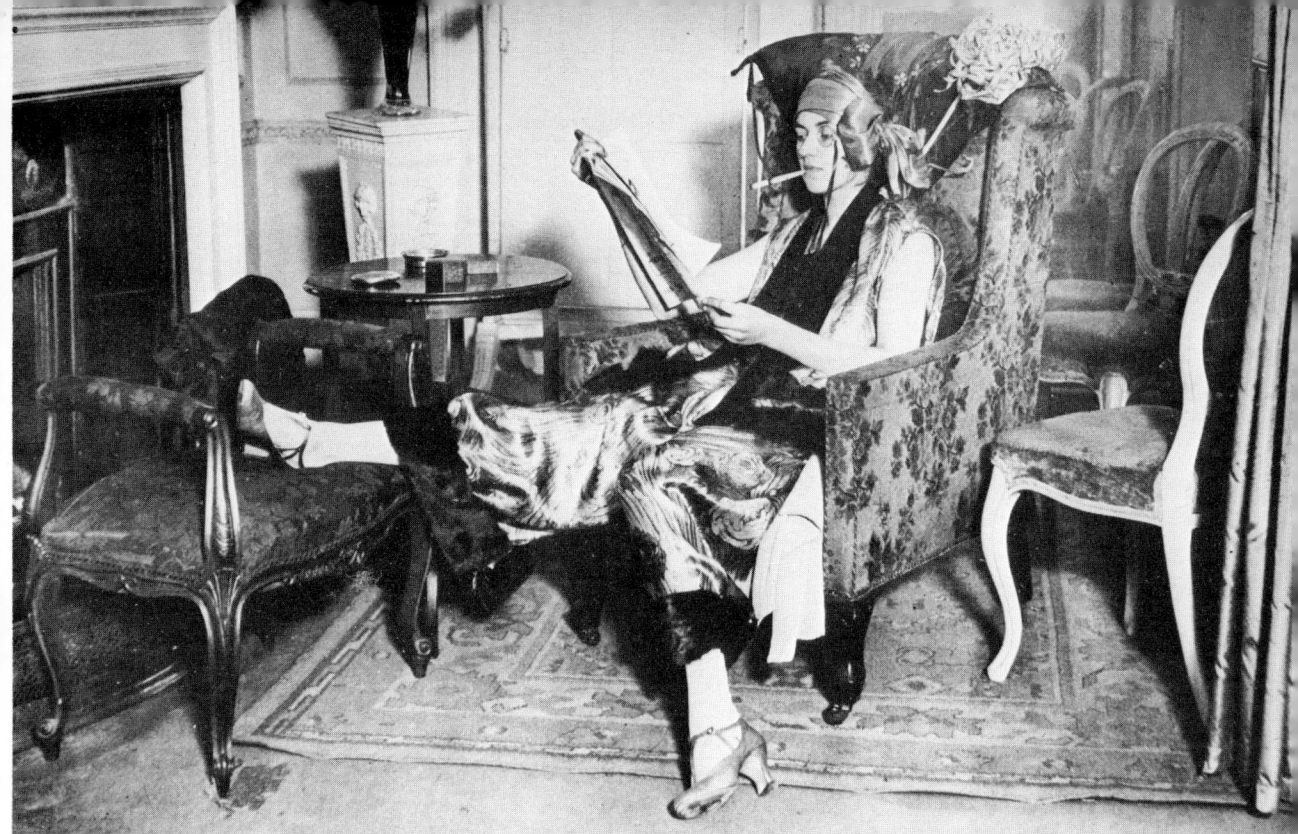

1922. A 'smoking suit'. The nonchalance, the cigarette in its holder, the monocle and all that expanse of ankle show great daring. No wonder some men ran a mile

A Norman Hartnell fashion in 1924

A 1927 fashion plate

The sixth Queen Charlotte's Birthday Ball—a highlight of the 'season'—and what was being worn at the preliminary committee meetings. The year 1933

acceptable, although a trained cook or parlour-maid could command almost double that.

Women enjoyed their new-found independence. In the early twenties, the frills and furbelows of pre-war days had been discarded. Hair was 'Eton cropped' or 'bobbed' and covered by the snug-fitting cloche hat. The straight up-and-down dresses did nothing for those with pretensions to any sort of figure.

Clothes made of rayon were not yet widely marketed. For the well-to-do it was silk stockings; for others, cotton or wool. After 1925 skirts, which had risen to above the knee, descended and the thirties saw a return to a more feminine elegance. The petticoat had

been discarded—with morals according to some people—in favour of the slip. The elastic belt replaced the corset; the first two-way-stretch belt appearing daringly on the market in the early thirties.

Going out to work was not confined to the working classes. Educated, middle-class women often found jobs and spent what they earned on clothes, smokes and drink. ('Have a Virgin, dear'—the proffered case containing Virginian and Turkish cigarettes.) They smoked and drank in public, flitted in open sports cars from cocktail party to cocktail party to evening party to early-morning party—or so their elders believed—and talked too loudly in exaggerated and affected voices. It was the thing to be *toujours gai*, to appear much more wicked than one really was.

The men were less adventurous—with clothes, anyhow. True, the wide 'Oxford' bags, light-coloured suits, cheerful ties and 'co-respondent' shoes (black-and-white or brown-and-white buckskin) were worn, but there was still a time and place for everything. The time and place were not in business hours or in business circles. The Civil Service would not have approved either. Nobody should appear conspicuous, so the conventional suit (often black jacket and black-and-grey striped trousers), white shirt, dark tie, bowler hat, stiff white collar (and probably stiff white cuffs) epitomised 'the City Gent'. Hair, of course, was short-back-and-sides.

In the street a gentleman, when accompanying a lady, still walked on the side nearest the roadway—a reminder of the days when a bolting horse might have mounted the pavement. In the house he still got up from his chair when she entered the room, and opened the door for her as she left. The well-mannered gentleman was subject to much bobbing up and down.

Going abroad was an adventure. 'Gay Paree'—with all the naughtiness that spelling implied—could be reached by Imperial Airways from Croydon Airport.

It was all great fun. But the thirties would be different.

EDUCATION AFTER the war was intended to be an improvement on the blatant class-distinction system of Edwardian times. H. A. L. Fisher, President of the Board of Education in 1917 and originator of the 1918 Education Act, planned compulsory full-time schooling up to the age of fourteen, and part-time education until at least sixteen. Nursery schools were to be encouraged and grants given to establish and run them. Unfortunately the Geddes Axe fell on much of this and the economic situation of the thirties further restricted Fisher's hopes.

His proposals on teachers' pay—subsequently known as the Burnham Scale—did attract responsive and intelligent teachers, and the standard was greatly improved—aided by BBC schools broadcasting.

The public schools flourished. The old-established ones clung to their ancient traditions which had little bearing on the changing modes and manners. New public schools such as Stowe and Canford (both opened in 1923 with a stiffening of senior pupils from the established institutions), and Bryanston (1928) had no archaic traditions to impede their progress. Boys did not need to wear a uniform designed in a previous century, or follow slavishly the worst features of the fagging system. There were also new progressive experiments such as A. S. Neill's school at Summerhill.

Since the war the influence of the Labour Party had been gaining ground. In 1924 the first Labour Government was formed under the leadership of Ramsay MacDonald. It lasted ten months. With the Conservatives dominating the Commons with 258 members to Labour's 191, the Liberals held the vital balance of power, with 158. Asquith believed Labour should be given a chance, and abhorred the prospect of joining the Protectionist Conservatives. As long as the Liberals went along with Labour the Government could survive. But MacDonald, hindered by inter-party quarrels, continual harassment from the Conservatives and the necessity to placate the Liberals before making controversial policy decisions, found the alliance impossible to maintain. The Labour Government found that it could not implement many of the reforms in which the party believed. However, more money was to be made available for education, that sad victim of Geddes. Money was found for public works in the hope that growing unemployment would be halted, and a more humane attitude towards unemployment and insurance payments became respectable.

But in a predominantly Conservative country (the party had polled over 5 million votes at the election, against Labour's 4 million) there was a growing suspicion of the Government's sympathy with communism. Labour's supporters even sang 'The Red Flag'. Its working-class origin and only very recent experience of government were not forgotten. There were dark fears that a Labour Government would confiscate property, nationalise industry and 'loosen morals'.

The formality of governmental procedure, the senseless dressing-up on state occasions, created difficulties and resentment. These were traditions of governments consisting of men of the Establishment, and the new masters—the labourer, the mill-hand, the engine-driver—found themselves ill at ease. Cartoonists cruelly depicted them coming to terms with the new way of life.

These 'class' aspects and the feared revolutionary tendencies contributed to the Government's downfall. Seditious articles had been appearing in the communist *Worker's Weekly* and its acting editor, J. R. Campbell, was arrested and charged under the 1797 Incitement to Mutiny Act. The case, however, was withdrawn on the basis that what had been written did not mean what was implied. This was too much for the Conservatives; it confirmed their suspicions of duplicity. Even Liberal support was alienated. The situation was not helped by Government mishandling in the Commons. MacDonald asked for a vote of confidence, but failed to get it.

The path was clear for a Conservative Government. Any obstacles were dramatically blasted by a substantial communist 'bogey'. A few days before polling date *The Times* uncovered a 'Soviet Plot'. A letter of the utmost secrecy, signed by Zinoviev of the Presidium of the Communist International, had been intercepted by the Foreign Office on its way to the British Communist Party. The letter urged the British Communists to foment trouble in the armed forces, to work for a treaty with Russia, and to watch the Labour Party leaders lest the taste of power and the better way of life engulfed them in the folds of the *bourgeoisie*.

Was the letter genuine or a fake? Charges and counter-charges abounded. Although the Conservatives would have won the election, the revealing 'Zinoviev letter' gave them a large majority. The waverers and 'don't-knows' played for safety and flocked to the stalwart Stanley Baldwin, with his pipe and broccoli; there was an Englishman you could trust. It was November 1924.

The Locarno Pact of 1925 was an important milestone in the attempt to regulate and secure relations between the powers. It guaranteed Germany's western frontiers and the demilitarisation of the Rhineland. Germany, Belgium and France agreed to settle differences without going to war. Britain and Italy undertook to aid the victims should the pact be broken.

At home the economic position was looking a little healthier, and after considerable discussion it was decided that Britain should return to the gold standard. This restored Britain's influence in the world money markets, but it overvalued the pound and helped create an inability to weather the stock-market crash of a few years later.

THE GENERAL STRIKE was the climax of industrial unrest—especially in the coal mines—that had been smouldering for years. The workers were disillusioned and considered the Conservatives had gained power by the trickery of the Zinoviev Letter. Unemployment and prices were still high. With the severe housing shortage and other real grievances, a breeding-ground for agitators existed. This unrest was brought to boiling point by the short-sightedness and the penny-pinching attitudes of some employers.

The preamble to the General Strike was the Government's decision in July 1925 to discontinue the subsidy to the coal industry. The mine-owners made their intentions clear: to cut wages, abolish the principle of a minimum wage and lengthen the working hours. A Government Commission agreed for the most part with the cuts proposed by the mine-owners

The General Strike, 1926: Bobby on a bus, barbed wire on the bonnet

and added that unprofitable pits should be closed. The labour movement combined to make a massive protest. A General Strike was threatened. The Labour Party, in opposition, although supporting the workers had grave doubts about the outcome of a General Strike. Passions might be difficult to control; there was a smell of revolution. The Government made emergency plans.

It was 'them' and 'us', the division of the 'haves' and 'have-nots'. The showdown had been reached; neither side could make concessions without seeming to yield on an important principle. The General Strike was called for 3 May 1926. The country woke that morning to find no transport whatsoever—not even a cruising taxi was to be seen. Life in the cities was virtually at a standstill. The power plants were taken over by the Government, and troops were ordered to maintain essential food supplies.

There were two sorts of people—union and non-union. The former withdrew into their shells except in the capacity of pickets and action against 'scabs', the latter were revitalised. The non-union contingent cast aside a lifetime of inhibitions and rallied to the support of the Government. The enthusiastic amateur came into his own. There was no lack of volunteers to unload ships, drive trains, lorries and buses. There was an eagerness to get things going again, and the middle classes, donning their sports clothes and overalls responded to the challenge. It was a matter of honour to show the Reds—and that embraced the workers— that they were not indispensable. Life could carry on without them and, my goodness, it was fun, old boy. Crash those gears, shift that

15

(*above*) *The General Strike, 1926: Milk was stored in Hyde Park*

(*below*) *The General Strike, 1926: Food convoy in Holborn*

The General Strike, 1926: Volunteer railway workers

coal, get a bit of steam up and land at Crewe (or wherever).

There were no newspapers except for the Government broadsheet *The British Gazette*; although the *Daily Mail* printed an edition in Paris which was flown to London. The BBC announced a steady stream of factual information and official instructions. The *Daily Herald* eventually managed to publish—with the aid of volunteers—a small daily newsheet, *The British Worker*, warning workers on strike of the attempts being made to break their spirit and solidarity.

On 13 May, the TUC called off the strike. The Government had declared a General Strike to be illegal, thus endangering union funds. The Government's legal position was, in fact, weaker than was believed at the time, and had it gone to court they might well have lost. But the unions were discouraged by inter-union disagreements and the realisation that the

nation's business had not collapsed, despite such a massive withdrawal of labour. So life returned to nearly normal, though the bitterness remained. The printers' and transport workers' unions kept their men out for a further five days in protest, and the miners did not return to work for six months. As their situation became desperate, the winter finally beat them into submission.

The Government had won. The amateur stevedores, bus and train drivers returned to their jobs. A *Punch* cartoon by Frank Reynolds showed a bored man in college blazer gazing flatly out of the french windows as his mother remarks to a friend, 'You see, he misses the strike so dreadfully.' To some it had been a trying interruption, to others an exhilarating tonic; but the distrust and suspicion arising from the General Strike was to last for generations.

A General Election was due in 1929. Un-

(*above*) *Scarcity in the midst of plenty; miners searching for coal in Wales.* (*below*) *General Election, 1929. Waiting for another 'Zinoviev letter'. Low's cartoon shows Winston Churchill, J. C. C. Davidson (Chairman of the Conservative Party Organisation), William Joynson-Hicks, and Stanley Baldwin in the hot seat*

"DEAR, DEAR! SURELY M? ZINOVIEV HASN'T MISSED THE POST!"

TURNING 'EM CORNER.

Strube's 'little man' perpetually turning the corner in search of better times. This cartoon appeared in the Daily Express *in 1929*

employment and peace were the issues; the debate was to be over which party could best deal with these problems. The Conservatives maintained that unemployment was not as serious as it seemed. 'Safety First', counselled Baldwin on the assumption, presumably, better the devil you know . . . Slum clearance, education and welfare benefits were also part of the Conservative manifesto. After the Zinoviev letter, each party was fearful of a stunt that would swing the electorate at the last moment, but it was an unexciting election and far from satisfactory. Labour was the largest party with 287 seats, the Conservatives had 261 and the Liberals could only muster 59. Once more the Liberals held the balance of power, and Ramsay

MacDonald returned as Prime Minister for the second time.

UNEMPLOYMENT (over 1 million) had marginally decreased when the new Government took office, and it continued to drop for the first six months, but in 1930, despite the favourable seasonal factors, it rose steadily to a staggering $2\frac{1}{2}$ million by the end of the year. The world monetary system was in chaos. Loans to Germany, the payment of war debts and the ability of financiers to take profits when and where they could, undermined any attempts to stabilise the international economy. The carrot of prosperity dangled in front of the American

=Wall Street Extra--Closing Prices=

THE WEATHER
Cloudy and Cooler
To-night and Tuesday
Detailed Weather Report on Page 16

The Evening Gazette

CLOSING STOCK PRICES

"THE PAPER THAT GOES HOME"

WORCESTER, MASS., MONDAY, OCTOBER 28, 1929. 30 PAGES TWO CENTS

SECOND MARKET CRASH DROPS PRICES $10-$50

TOTAL STOCK SALES 9,199,700 SHARES

Another terrific nose dive—Final quotations around low levels of day—Heavy liquidation set in when market opened, but was halted temporarily when buying by banking pool appeared—U. S. Steel broke to $186, net loss of $17.50.

By STANLEY W. PRENOSIL
Associated Press Financial Editor

NEW YORK, Oct. 28 (AP)—The stock market went into another terrific nose-dive today, breaking through the low levels established in last Thursday's record-breaking session. As prices of scores of leading issues crashed $10 to nearly $50 a share, with final quotations around the low levels of the day, net declines in

NO RALLY AT END OF TODAY'S MARKET CRASH

Losses Much Larger Than Last Thursday and Closing Was Much Weaker—Prices Left Off at Bottom

2,884,300 SHARES IN LAST 50 MINUTES

By GEORGE T. HUGHES
By Special Leased Wire to The Gazette
WALL STREET, NEW YORK, Oct. 28—Wall Street experienced today its second price crash within a week. Compared with last Thursday, the losses were much larger and the closing was much weaker.

There was no rally at the end today as there had been on Thursday. Prices left off at the bottom.

MANY FAVORITES AT YEAR'S LOW

In today's violent plunge of the market, low points for the year were established in many of the issues which a short time ago were grazing the peaks with enthusiastic speculators pushing for even higher levels. Of this selected list of 30 stocks which have been in the van during the past few months, 23 today rested at the lowest points in 1929:

	Year's High	Year's Low	Today's Close
American Can	184½	107⅝	136
Am. & For. Power	199¼	73½	75
Am. Smelting	108¼	88½	90
Am. Tel. & Tel.	310¼	198¼	232
Anaconda	174⅞	92	98½
Andes Copper	68⅝	42	40¼
Atlantic Refining	77⅞	40	40⅝
Baltimore & Ohio	145½	115¼	115½
Barnsdall A	49½	20⅞	22¼
Beth. Steel	140⅝	82½	94½
Briggs Mfg.	68⅞	13½	13⅝
Can. Pacific	265⅞	200	203
Cerro de Pasco	120	80	77½
Chrysler	135	48	40
Col. Gas & El.	140	58½	70⅝
Columbia Graph.	88⅝	27½	23¾
Comwlth & South.	24¾	18	15
Consol. Gas	183½	95½	97¼
Erie	93½	60	55
Gen. El.	403	219	230
Gen. Foods	81½	30	48¼
Gen. Motors	91¾	40	47½
Gold Dust	82	45	40
Hudson Motors	93½	60½	60
Johns-Manville	242⅞	140	122

ENDORSED FOR JUDGE OF DISTRICT COURT

Photo by J. Carroll Brown
JUDGE FRANK L. RILEY

The question of a successor to Judge Samuel Utley as presiding justice of

LOOK INTO STORY OF STOLEN GIRL

Chief Requests Mayor to Suspend Patrolman, Pending Further Investigation by Police Authorities of Claim That Autoist Was Ousted From His Own Machine by Officer in Uniform Who Then Drove Off With Fair Companion

Following charges that a uniformed patrolman ousted Worcester man from his brand-new automobile and disappeared with the car and Ida May Savaria of 133 Franklin street, his companion, Chief of Police Foley stated today that he had partially completed an inquiry and was forwarding charges to Mayor O'Hara, asking for the suspension of Patrolman John F. [illegible] of Station 1.

Shortly after the request for the patrolman's suspension was received from Chief Foley, Mayor O'Hara ordered his clerks to make out the necessary

CITY PATROLMAN UNDER SUSPENSION

public was worm-eaten. Unrealistically inflated market prices, the eagerness of all to buy at such prices created a field-day for the unscrupulous. What went up must come down and never was that truer than of the American stock market. As the market turned and plummeted to its new level, confidence collapsed and many of the banks with it. Thousands of small investors in America were left holding a mass of worthless, or near worthless, paper securities—the remains of their savings. America's economic collapse pulled the carpet from under the feet of the other nations who staggered and toppled trying to stand firm. Britain's trade with America sank, there were a series of financial crises and unemployment rose above $2\frac{1}{2}$ million. The Depression years had come.

Over 2 million unemployed could not be hidden. From all parts of Britain their representatives marched to London bringing a million-signature petition to present to parliament, demanding that work-schemes should be initiated in the depressed areas, and the 'means' test abolished. From Cardiff, Plymouth, Liverpool and other cities they marched, gaunt and drab, sleeping in village halls and workhouses on the way. In the comfortable middle-class areas, their arrival *en route* was a visible condemnation of the policies of successive governments. The marchers were welcomed into London by some 100,000 workers. Incidents in Hyde Park and Trafalgar Square necessitated baton charges by the police and some of the marchers' leaders were arrested and imprisoned.

Opinions, courses of action, appraisals—there was no lack of these in government and city circles; but there was little resolute action and what action there was came too late or was ineffective. A political crisis in August 1931 brought matters to a head. During the long parliamentary summer recess there was a flurry of activity out of which emerged a coalition National Government with Ramsay MacDonald leading an all-party cabinet.

Philip Snowden, Chancellor of the Exchequer, confronted with an estimated deficit of £74 million in the current year and an estimated deficit of £170 million in the next full year, increased taxation, abandoned the sacred cow of the gold standard and cut salaries of the government-employed. Judges, members of parliament, teachers, the police and the armed forces took pay cuts. Unemployment benefit also suffered. There were few items of government expenditure that were not drastically curtailed and although some kind of budget balance might have been achieved, the Government seemed powerless to stem the world monetary crisis in which Britain was so heavily involved.

The cuts in the forces' pay provoked a strike by naval ratings at Invergordon. Its seriousness was played down by the authorities who dismissed, rather than court martialled, the apparent ringleaders. But the incident could not be played down abroad, and sensational accounts published in the overseas press represented British institutions on the verge of collapse. Foreign investment fled the country and the financial situation grew worse.

There was growing pressure for another election to give the National Government a mandate, which they received in November

Mutinous ratings. On board the Hood *at Invergordon, 1931*

Britain's destiny between-the-wars was largely in the hands of these politicians. The photograph is of the first National Government, 1931. Left to right, back row: Sir P. Cunliffe-Lister (Board of Trade), J. H. Thomas (Dominions), Lord Reading (Foreign Office), Neville Chamberlain (Health), Sir Samuel Hoare (India). Front row: Philip Snowden (Chancellor of the Exchequer), Stanley Baldwin (Lord President), Ramsay MacDonald (Prime Minister), Sir Herbert Samuel (Home Office), Lord Sankey (Lord Chancellor)

1931. The result was 556 seats for the National Government; 59 seats for the Opposition. Ramsay MacDonald continued as Prime Minister but was clearly a prisoner of the Conservative majority. Baldwin was Lord President of the Council and Sir John Simon, the Liberal leader, was appointed Foreign Secretary.

Within a month of taking office the new Government was involved with the Manchurian crisis. The Chinese appealed to the League of Nations over the Japanese invasion, but conflicting interests and delays resulted in the League's first defeat. It was powerless to offer a solution and what had initially been a border incident became, with the fighting in Shanghai, a full-scale war. Gunboat diplomacy by the American Navy and conventional diplomatic activity by Britain secured an uneasy truce, but did not end the war. Japan withdrew from the League and continued her aggression against China unhindered. The war was remote from Britain and the fighting continued spasmodically until it merged with the greater conflict in the forties.

BY 1935 the nations were recovering from their economic sickness. Production and international trade began to pick up. A fall in world commodity prices brought cheaper imports to Britain. Export prices remained relatively high, and so some hundreds of millions could be saved. The successive governments had tried to cure the economic malaise by the old method of retrenchment, but with little success. The eventual lifting of the Depression gave confirmation to the new concept of economic planning, and especially to John Maynard Keynes's revolution in economic theory.

The distressed areas where unemployment was highest (Jarrow, in 1934, had 67·8 per cent of its insured workers unemployed) could only be helped on a national scale. Hunger marches, reports from outside bodies and independent surveys shamed the Government into action. In November 1934 a bill was introduced providing for unpaid commissioners to initiate schemes for the economic development and social improvement of the depressed areas. Industries were encouraged to establish themselves in these areas and every assistance was given with ready-made factories and financial concessions. The industrial estates at Treforest in South Wales, Team Valley near Gateshead, and North Hillingdon near Glasgow date from this time. The number of unemployed did fall, although not entirely owing to these development policies. The labour force was now more mobile and moved to areas and jobs where there was work. Rearmament, later in the thirties, gave the much needed boost to the sluggish heavy industries of steel, iron and shipbuilding.

Marina was a popular name for girls born at this time

THE DUKE AND DUCHESS OF KENT WAVING TO THE ENTHUSIASTIC THRONG FROM THE BALCONY OF BUCKINGHAM PALACE

So the Depression was over. Unemployment figures were declining and the international crises of the future years were not yet apparent to all. Some relaxation was called for; a little window dressing perhaps, some pomp and ceremony. It came in the form of the marriage in December 1934 of Prince George (King George V's fourth son, later the Duke of Kent) to Princess Marina of Greece. A fairy story romance helped to divert attention from the realities of life. The press coverage was impressive—with special supplements with photographs of the handsome couple. The instinctive fashion sense of the beautiful princess was a spur to the rag trade and a bonanza for the shops.

This was followed the next year by the Silver Jubilee of King George V and Queen Mary, an occasion for rejoicing and dancing in the streets. Members of Parliament, scurrying from one social function to the next, all smiles, realised that this was the time for a General Election. Better now, they thought, before the electorate's loyalty and patriotism waned. The election took place in June and the Conservatives, with National Liberal and National Labour members, had an overall majority of nearly 250. It was a hard-fought election. The patriotism and loyalty had rubbed off a bit. Ramsay MacDonald was defeated at Seaham by 20,000 votes, although he reached the Commons by the back door as a member for the Scottish Universities. His reputation was discredited. His Labour image had been badly tarnished by his association with what had been virtually a Conservative government. He now seemed no longer capable of holding high office, and he was replaced as Prime Minister by Stanley Baldwin.

To the electorate it must have appeared to be more or less the same old gang, shuffled around. A few new faces here and there, a few old men kicked upstairs to the Lords. But the smiles, the acclamations, the make-believe and the platitudes were coming to an end. There was a need for statesmen rather than politicians, and the former were in short supply. The rumblings of war could now be heard clearly, but there were only a few prepared to listen.

WORLD PEACE now depended on satisfying the apparently insatiable, power-hungry dictators, Hitler and Mussolini. Both men, with a fine sense of timing and displays of shouting, fawning, cajoling (depending on the circumstances) played off one European Power against the other, until they had achieved what they wanted without having to fight for it. The Powers huddled for comfort in the embrace of the League of Nations, but the actions taken by the dictators were quick and efficient and each time the League was presented with a *fait accompli*. The machinery of the League—speeches, lobbying, votes—was ponderous and its weapons—sanctions and condemnation—ineffective. The International Force that was to be deployed under the auspices of the League and sent to trouble spots never materialised.

The burning of the Reichstag building on the night of 27 February 1933 had heralded the arrival of Nazi power. It gave Hitler the opportunity to set aside the constitution and rule by decree. In 1935 a plebiscite was held in the Saar district under the auspices of the League of Nations. The choice for the Saar electorate was between remaining with the French who had worked the coalfields since the end of the war, or 'returning' to Germany. Hitler made sure of the answer and the Saar voted overwhelmingly to return to Germany. Neither this event, nor the introduction of conscription in Germany in March 1936 roused more than protests from the League. Step by step, Hitler was undermining the settlement of Versailles.

Mussolini in Italy took interested note of what Hitler was managing to achieve. Schemes of imperial glory and territorial gain in Africa had attracted Italy for some time. Mussolini's conquest of Abyssinia followed a pattern that was to become familiar by the end of the decade. First, the border skirmishes, and Abyssinia's protest to the League. Then a commission of inquiry set up by the League, followed by bargaining and compromise in the hope of placating the aggressor with something short of his full demands.

But Italian forces were already bound for East Africa. In order to halt the seemingly inevitable bloodshed, a plan was put to Mussolini by Sir Samuel Hoare, Britain's Foreign Secretary, with the help of Pierre Laval of France. The plan virtually handed over Abyssinia to Mussolini; but before it became fact the details were revealed in the press and such an outcry followed that Hoare was compelled to resign. Abyssinia was invaded and the League applied sanctions (except on oil and petrol, of which the Italians were woefully short). Italy's use of a mechanised army and aircraft against defenceless Abyssinians shocked the world. The Italian victory was a foregone conclusion, and—the final irony—the conquest was officially recognised.

HOWEVER MUCH the rumblings of war could be heard elsewhere in the world, there arose in Britain a constitutional crisis to which the Government had to give its undivided attention.

On the mantelpieces of many homes in Britain and the Empire, and above the desks of typists in innumerable offices was a photograph of Edward, Prince of Wales—the most popular one of him was in naval uniform, laughing and youthful. He was the embodiment of their ideal of an Englishman: dashing and handsome, with just the right degree of reticence and shyness. Not only in Britain was he popular. Even the Germans referred to him as 'prince' and liked to stress his links with them. The Americans hero-worshipped him. When, in January 1936, King George V died at Sandringham after a long illness, the nation mourned him and acclaimed his bachelor son, Edward, as their new king. Would, people asked, the conventions of royal behaviour be swept aside, or would King Edward VIII be tamed into submission by the Establishment? As Prince of Wales his

verbal anger at the conditions existing in the depressed areas, had been an embarrassment to those in power.

The king's friendship with Mrs Wallis Simpson was known to many, but was kept from the public. The reticence of the British press was the result of an agreement not to attack royalty or write about its lapses. The foreign press had no such scruples, and those in Britain who had access to foreign journals read of a situation that had all the makings of a constitutional crisis. When the *News Chronicle* revealed that a Mrs Simpson was obtaining a divorce from her husband at Ipswich, it meant little to the public at large, although it must have been difficult to account for the massive attendance of journalists (many American) at this undefended, and seemingly unremarkable, hearing.

In the higher echelons its importance was realised. An emergency cabinet meeting under Stanley Baldwin in November discussed the implications of the divorce and determined to keep the public in the dark. However, they were put in the picture by the *Yorkshire Post* which commented on some pertinent remarks by the Bishop of Bradford, Dr A. W. F. Blunt. At last

The Prince of Wales sees for himself

The Duke of Windsor marries

it dawned upon the population that the king had every intention of marrying the divorced Mrs Simpson.

For a week the country was in a turmoil. Some respected the king's feelings and thought that he should marry the woman of his choice, while others—the majority—thought otherwise. 'She don't seem to be the right sort of Queen. No class, as you might say. Not like Queen Mary,' commented a workman, and he voiced the attitude of many. The views of the Dominions and the Colonies had to be respected. For them distance did not lend enchantment. The traditions of royalty were very strong, and it was felt that the monarchy itself was at stake.

In Britain the factions were forming—the 'King's Friends', and those who were not his friends. Meanwhile the Establishment was busy. Meetings here and there, a word in the right quarter, a nod to the right person—all this against a background of public concern. On 10 December, in a crowded House of Commons, Stanley Baldwin handed to the Speaker a message from the king, signed by his own hand and witnessed by his brothers Albert, Henry and George, announcing his intention to abdicate. On the following day, as a private citizen, Edward broadcast a speech. In homes all over the world, people huddled round their sets listening. Rarely can there have been a more emotional few minutes. 'But you must believe me when I tell you that I have found it impossible to carry the heavy burden of responsibility and to discharge my duties as king as *I* would wish to do without the help and support of the woman I love . . .'

He then embarked for France and married Mrs Simpson the following year. He had reigned for 325 days. The following May (1937) George VI's Coronation took place, Baldwin went to the House of Lords and Neville Chamberlain became Prime Minister.

THE SPANISH CIVIL WAR in 1936 was a dress rehearsal for the World War that was to follow three years later. The liberal and left-wing actions of the Spanish Government had caused the right-wing parties concern. General Franco, with troops from Morocco under his command, attempted a *coup* which was initially unsuccessful. Had the Spaniards been left to fight it out amongst themselves the course of history might have been different. An appeal by the Spanish Government to the League of Nations achieved nothing. Help was sought from—and given by—Russia.

A communist-dominated Spain was an impossible strategic situation for the Axis powers. They supplied arms and technical help but despite all the evidence were reluctant to confess their involvement. The Russians, they maintained, were responsible for turning Spain into a battleground. What had begun as a civil war developed into a big-power confrontation, in which each tested its newly-developed weapons of war and calculatingly noted the effects on a defenceless people.

In Britain, feeling was intense. Opinion was split between Fascism (Germany and Italy) and Communism (Russia), and all the differences that followed such a division— totalitarianism, class, religion, democracy. The war assumed a symbolic importance. It was seen as part of the world-wide conflict that was increasingly dominating the minds of people in Britain. At last in the battlefields of Spain could be found some active means of fighting the fascist menace. Young people from all sections of the community joined the International Brigade in defence, not so much of Spain, but of their principles. Here the battle against aggression and totalitarianism was being fought.

General Franco won, and as victor he received recognition from the Powers; Spain was safe from communism. The Axis Powers having studied the strategy employed during the war and assessed the worthiness or otherwise of the military equipment used, were now prepared for further ventures. It had been relatively easy for them. Hitler, with intuitive skill had set the pace. He dragged Mussolini with him, the latter showing what independence he could,

Spanish Civil War. Fascist troops

It's never too soon . . .

. . . to learn

Britain-at-peace. Fascists acclaim Mosley

but remaining very much the junior partner. Dazzled by Hitler's success and more and more involved in Hitler's strategic plans for conquest, he did as he was told.

Germany was re-arming in the certain knowledge that such action would be met only by protests, but up to 1936 Hitler's successes had been confined to German territory, or to territory that had been Germany's before the 1914 War. Austria was outside Germany and its annexation was desirable in Hitler's eyes. If this could be achieved under the guise of diplomacy, all the better. The Austrians, it could be argued, *were* Germans. Surely such a small country should be under the 'protection' of the Reich? The pattern of Hitler's 'diplomacy' was to become familiar.

Schuschnigg, the Austrian Chancellor, was summoned to Berchtesgaden, an ultimatum was presented with the choice of submission or invasion. At the same time, Nazi agitators were creating disorder and demonstrations in Austria. Schuschnigg made a vain attempt to organise a referendum 'for' or 'against' the Reich's 'protection'. His attempt sealed Austria's fate. 'Referendum' was not a word in Hitler's book. His armies marched and Austria's incorporation into the Reich was accomplished.

Mussolini had watched the invasion of Austria, so close to his borders, with growing anxiety. He mistrusted Hitler, although he was an ally. Wisely, he remained silent. 'Tell Mussolini I will never forget him,' shouted Hitler with obvious relief. 'Never, never, never.' And he added for good measure, 'Whatever happens.'

'Whatever happens . . .' It was realised now by most people in Britain that events were rushing to a climax and that war would break out. With each successive 'territorial demand' by Hitler and the continuous warlike noises coming from his partner Mussolini, the word 'crisis' was becoming commonplace. When a crisis was anticipated, it became actual (generally at a weekend when senior civil servants and politicians were not readily available) and was over so quickly that no proper assessment of policy was possible. Thus, step by step, Hitler worked through his plan. The British looked on with impotent fury. 'Appeasement' would not work, could not work, but it seemed too late for any other policy except war. However, in certain circles there was still an admiration for the skill, timing and policies of the dictators.

Hitler's persecution of the Jews had resulted, from 1933, in their exodus from Germany. Their arrival in Britain created problems of assimilation. In appearance and behaviour the Jews were unacceptable to many. Their instinctive ability to overcome the difficulties of language and to make their influence felt in the business community, created jealousy. Why should Britain, it was argued, harbour those for whom Hitler had no use? Unemployment was rife, and there were thousands of the middle-class in dead-end jobs, offering little prospect of advancement. It could be seen that Hitler's unwanted people were not doing so badly. They may have reached Britain only in the clothes they stood up in, but inside the pockets were valuables that could be, and were, realised for cash. The money formed a sound basis on which to build life anew. The Jews knew how to make money work for them: most Britons did not.

Oswald Mosley's black-shirted British Union of Fascists attracted a considerable number of frustrated young men, and by 1934, the mem-

(left) Semi-detached house in the Coppice Estate, Lower Willingdon, near Eastbourne, Sussex. Typical of the 1937 period. (right) A page from the estate agent's brochure. No garage, but space for one. In the kitchen an electric clock. Or you might prefer a 'delightfully cosy' semi-detached bungalow for £575 (£25 down and 15s a week)

£625 FREEHOLD.

SEMI-DETACHED 3 BEDROOM HOUSE

Distinctive and Compact. .

ACCOMMODATION.

GROUND FLOOR.

LOUNGE: 12ft. 6ins. by 10ft. 9ins.
DINING ROOM: 10ft. 6ins. by 10ft. with French Windows leading to Garden.
Tiled KITCHEN, with bay window and fitted with Electric Clock. Good LARDER.
Outside FUEL STORE and w.c. (with covered access).
Nice HALL, with side window.
Large GARDEN.   Space for GARAGE.

FIRST FLOOR.

BEDROOM 1: 11ft. 10ins. by 10ft. 4ins., with bay.
BEDROOM 2: 12ft. 1in. by 9ft.
BEDROOM 3: 8ft. by 8ft.
Tiled BATHROOM, with w.c.

INSTALMENT TERMS.

From £35 inclusive deposit, then **XXX** per week for 23 years.

16/1 — 6/1

See illustration in centre of book.

Page seven

(*left*) *Enter for safety, with gas masks handy.* (*right*) *Exit for safety. Children being evacuated to the country, 1939*

bership was in the region of 20,000. Meetings and marches in areas where the Jews lived provoked scenes of disorder and violence. New legislation was necessary to curb it, and this, coupled with the rise of Fascism in Germany which was by 1937 recognised as the common enemy, prevented it becoming a serious challenge.

Nevertheless, in the higher echelons of society the Nazi regime was not without admirers. Cliveden, the Astor country estate, was said to be the meeting-place for the socially acceptable with pro-Nazi sympathies. Ribbentrop, who was then German ambassador, entertained lavishly the influential and susceptible who might further the German cause. He had not been in the convivial champagne business for nothing.

The man-in-the-street, standing between the vocal Left and the influential Right, had few illusions. The post-war promises had not worked out. Britain was different, but not necessarily better. Class distinction seemed even more marked. Wealth was in the hands of the few;

poverty was the lot of too many. The slums had not been cleared; although there were the new suburbs with their neat semi-detached houses, complete with handkerchief-sized gardens carefully tended by proud owners. Factories looking like exhibition buildings were erected on the new motor roads which carried the ever-increasing spate of cars to the coasts. The cinema flourished. People flocked to the new picture palaces, garish and glittering. Hollywood stars were now the leaders of fashion, and their behaviour, romances and way of life were revealed in the newspapers and magazines, to be lapped up by the public.

If the twenties were carefree, it was in the thirties that people's social consciences were aroused. The formation of societies and welfare organisations to help the underprivileged point to a less indifferent attitude to suffering. If many such societies had a strong left-wing bias, this was because, over the years, the political differences had become much more marked, and the Spanish Civil War had done much to accentuate this.

Was war inevitable? Perhaps Hitler did mean what he said. Give him just this and it *would* be his last territorial claim in Europe. Germany could not be kept under for ever. She had a claim, after nearly quarter of a century, to have some rights. Hitler's tactics? The brutality and the concentration camps? Surely not as bad as reported. We must live our lives; others must live theirs and the British way of life was not for everyone, more's the pity. The tendency was to push away unpleasantness and to ignore the facts. Hitler's tactics were the stick and the carrot. It was the carrot that was gobbled up; it is the stick that is remembered now.

HITLER'S NEXT stick was Czechoslovakia. He demanded that the Sudeten German districts should be ceded to Germany. The situation was particularly critical because German aggression in that direction would involve France and, by implication, Britain. For Chamberlain, appeasement was the only policy. Twice he flew to see Hitler at Berchtsesgaden, the latter's demands increasing on the second occasion. At the later Munich meeting on 29 September 1938, Chamberlain and Daladier on the one side, Hitler and Mussolini on the other, drew up a plan that was passed to the waiting representatives of Dr Benes, President of Czechoslovakia. The Sudetenland was to be given to Germany. The plan virtually crippled Czechoslovakia's prosperity and safety, as her massive ring of defences and important industrial region were handed over to Germany. No argument or protest by Czechoslovakia would be tolerated. Hitler had what he wanted without a shot fired. Czechoslovakia had been betrayed, and Britain and France had been party to that betrayal.

When Chamberlain returned to Britain, he had with him a signed paper from Hitler agreeing to settle all future disputes by consultation and to renounce war. 'Peace in our time', Chamberlain said. That time was short, and with Czechoslovakia out of action Poland lay exposed.

WAR HAD been averted. The hastily-dug trenches in the parks were filled in, the sandbags emptied and stacked, the Air Raid Precautions put aside, the gas masks stowed away. The children returned from the safety of the country to their homes in the cities. Mingled with relief was indignation. Mass Observation's report on Britain testifies to the unease and guilt. 'I used to be proud to be British, but now I'm ashamed of my own race', and 'We've let them down', meaning the Czechs; though Godfrey Winn in the *Sunday Express* could say 'Praise be to God and to Mr. Chamberlain. I had no sacrilege, no bathos, in coupling those two names.'

Any doubts in people's minds about the inevitability of war were dispelled, as Hitler, in March 1939, completed the conquest of Czechoslovakia by occupying Prague. Now no small country was safe from his attention. Rumania next, perhaps, with its oil so necessary for the German war effort?

In May 1939, in an atmosphere of mutual distrust, the British and French governments discussed with Russia the possibilities of a pact of mutual assistance. Russia, looking after her own interests and realising the possible futility of the Franco-British negotiations, carried on parallel negotiations with Germany. In August, a Russo-German commercial agreement was signed, a sinister preliminary to the treaty on 23 August which produced a non-aggression pact for ten years and secretly determined Germany's and Russia's spheres of influence in a carved-up Europe. The Allies retired, hurt. The Russo-German treaty was the final irony. The sworn enemies had come together. Russia could observe in safety, sure of her pickings. Hitler was free to employ his forces in Europe without interference from his eastern flank.

It was Poland, now horribly exposed by Germany's conquest of Czechoslovakia, that revealed to Chamberlain the threat to peace and discredited the policy of appeasement. He announced that Britain felt herself 'bound at once to lend the Polish Government all support . . .' France, who had a military alliance with

The Daily Telegraph

and Morning Post

LATE LONDON EDITION

NO. 26,288   LONDON, MONDAY, SEPTEMBER 4, 1939   BROADCASTING—Page Six   ONE PENNY

GREAT BRITAIN AT WAR

THE KING'S MESSAGE TO THE EMPIRE

MR. CHURCHILL FIRST LORD: POST FOR MR. EDEN

PREMIER SETS UP WAR CABINET

VISCOUNT GORT TO COMMAND FIELD FORCE

The Prime Minister announced yesterday in a message broadcast to the Empire, that as from 11 o'clock in the morning, Great Britain is at war with Germany.

The Commonwealth of Australia proclaimed a state of war three hours later, New Zealand followed and France was at war from 5 o'clock in the afternoon. Canada has given an assurance of effective co-operation.

The House of Commons met at noon to hear from Mr. Chamberlain the declaration that Britain was at war.

In the Lords a similar announcement was made by Lord Halifax. M.P.s will meet again to-day at 3 o'clock.

PREMIER SEES THE KING

At 6 o'clock in the evening the King broadcast a rallying call to the Empire. An hour later Mr. Chamberlain had an audience of his Majesty.

It was later announced that the Prime Minister has established a War Cabinet, consisting of eight members in addition to himself.

WAR CABINET OF NINE

MR. CHURCHILL BACK AT ADMIRALTY

MINISTER OF HOME SECURITY

A War Cabinet of nine has been set up on the lines of that established in December, 1916. It was announced from No. 10, Downing-street last night that the King had approved its constitution as follows:

PRIME MINISTER AND FIRST LORD OF THE TREASURY: Mr. Neville Chamberlain.

CHANCELLOR OF THE EXCHEQUER: Sir John Simon.

SECRETARY OF STATE FOR FOREIGN AFFAIRS: Viscount Halifax.

MINISTER FOR CO-ORDINATION OF DEFENCE: Adml. of the Fleet Lord Chatfield.

FIRST LORD OF THE ADMIRALTY: Mr. Winston Churchill.

SECRETARY OF STATE FOR WAR: Mr. Leslie Hore-Belisha.

SECRETARY OF STATE FOR AIR: Sir Kingsley Wood.

Mr. Churchill replaces Earl Stanhope as First Lord of the Admiralty and Sir Samuel Hoare replaces Sir John Anderson as Lord Privy Seal.

OUTSIDE THE CABINET

Later it was announced from Downing-street that the King's approval had also been given to the following appointments of Ministers not in the War Cabinet:

LORD PRESIDENT OF THE COUNCIL: Earl Stanhope (formerly First Lord of the Admiralty).

LORD CHANCELLOR: Sir Thomas Inskip (formerly Dominion Secretary).

SECRETARY OF STATE FOR THE HOME DEPARTMENT AND MINISTER OF HOME SECURITY: Sir John Anderson (formerly Lord Privy Seal).

SECRETARY OF STATE FOR DOMINION AFFAIRS: Mr. Anthony Eden.

Mr. Eden is to have special access to the Cabinet in order to be in the best position to maintain contact between it and the Dominions.

Lord Hankey, who is 62, was better known as Sir Maurice Hankey, until he

BRITISH FLEET BEGINS THE BLOCKADE

Shipping Liable To Examination

HIS MAJESTY'S BROADCAST

The following message was broadcast by the King from Buckingham Palace throughout the Empire at 6 o'clock last evening:

In this grave hour, perhaps the most fateful in our history, I send to every household of my peoples, both at home and overseas, this message, spoken with the same depth of feeling for each one of you as if I were able to cross your threshold and speak to you myself.

For the second time in the lives of most of us we are at war. Over and over again we have tried to find a peaceful way out of the differences between ourselves and those who are now our enemies. But it has been in vain.

We have been forced into a conflict. For we are called, with our Allies, to meet the challenge of a principle which, if it were to prevail, would be fatal to any civilised order in the world.

It is the principle which permits a State, in the selfish pursuit of power, to disregard its treaties and its solemn pledges; which sanctions the use of force, or threat of force, against the Sovereignty and independence of other States.

Such a principle, stripped of all disguise, is surely the mere primitive doctrine that might is right; and if this principle were established throughout the world, the freedom of our own country and of the whole British Commonwealth of Nations would be in danger.

But far more than this — the peoples of the world would be kept in the bondage of fear, and all hopes of settled peace and of the security of justice and liberty among nations would be ended.

This is the ultimate issue which confronts us. For the sake of all that we ourselves hold dear, and of the world's order and peace, it is unthinkable that we should refuse to meet the challenge.

It is to this high purpose that I now call my people at home and my peoples across the Seas, who will make our cause their own.

I ask them to stand calm, firm and united in this time of trial. The task will be hard. There may be dark days ahead, and war can no longer be confined to the battlefield. But we can only do the right as we see the right, and reverently commit our cause to God.

If one and all we keep resolutely faithful to it, ready for whatever service or sacrifice it may demand, then, with God's help, we shall prevail.

May He bless and keep us all.

DOMINIONS AT WAR

AUSTRALIA AND NEW ZEALAND

Australia and New Zealand yesterday declared war on Germany in support of the action of Great Britain. The Canadian Cabinet met for two

FIERCE FIGHTING ON TWO POLISH SECTORS

MANY WEEK-END RAIDS BY GERMAN WARPLANES

THRUST INTO EAST PRUSSIA CLAIMED IN WARSAW

Fighting on a more extensive scale is developing on both the main fronts in Poland.

The German attempt to cut the Corridor between Chojnice and Graudenz was reported in Warsaw last night to have failed. At the same time it was stated that the Poles had recovered certain of their towns in this zone and had penetrated across the border into East Prussia.

Further air raids were made on Polish towns over the week-end. A Polish Foreign Office statement estimates that 1,500, including women and children, have been killed and wounded by bombing since Friday.

Below are messages from our special correspondents in Warsaw and Katowice.

POLES CHEER DECLARATIONS

FROM OUR SPECIAL CORRESPONDENT

WARSAW, Sunday.

The Germans occupied Rybnik, Teschen, Fryntat, and have reached the suburbs of Katowice. They are pouring in by the Moravian Gate to cut communications between Katowice and Crakow.

Constant raids occurred at Crakow to-day.

The civilian population has evacuated Katowice. From Crakow heavy rifle and artillery fire is heard from all along the frontier.

The German minority indulged in sabotage and espionage in this area and cut all telephone lines from

who appeared was lifted into the air by students.

The next objective of the crowd was the British Consulate, where the Consul, Mr. P. Savery, one of the most popular figures in Poland, appeared on the balcony, waving a huge Union Jack amid deafening cheers.

A spokesman in the crowd, knowing English, cried: "Long live Great Britain and King George; long live British democracy and 20th-century civilisation."

WARSAW RAIDED

Warsaw had constant raid alarms after dawn to-day. I heard heavy

---

Poland, was party to the pledge. Quite how Britain, geographically situated as she was, could have assisted Poland is not clear, but Hitler was prepared to put it to the test. Feverish activity by the Powers to satisfy Hitler's demands without actually giving in to them were of no avail. Even his ally Mussolini, fearful of the consequences of war for which he was ill-prepared, endeavoured to influence his partner; but it was too late.

For Hitler, the Russo-German pact was the final piece that fitted his jigsaw of aggression. At a quarter to five on the morning of 1 September 1939, the German army invaded Poland. On 3 September 1939 at 11 am Britain and Germany were at war. Fifteen minutes later Neville Chamberlain broadcast to the nation. His listeners, huddled round their wireless sets, heard another sound while he was speaking; the wail of the air-raid siren.

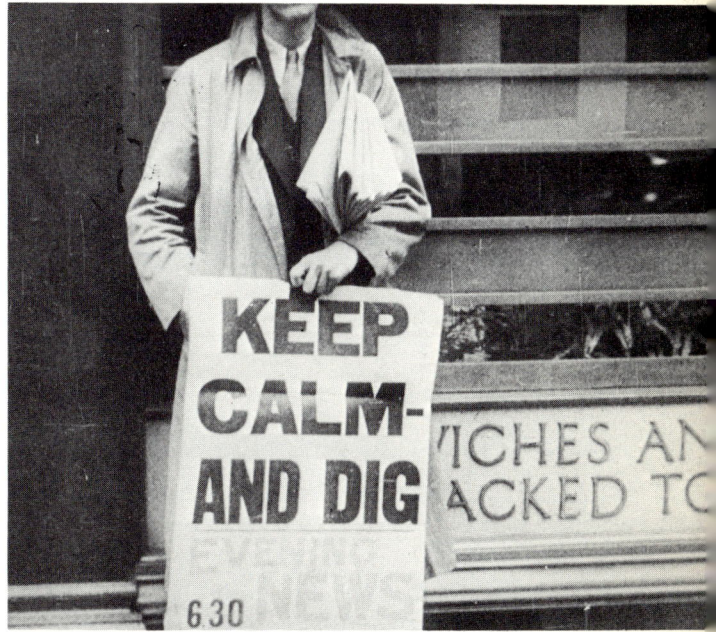

HAVE YOU FORGOTTEN YET?

FOR MANY the period between the two World Wars is sharply defined. It is twenty years that falls neatly into place between two shattering events, the 'long weekend' as it has been called. A time of high hopes, but of disappointments, of great social change and adjustment. For those who lived through the period, it is not necessarily the 'great events' that stand out.

A tune, a photograph, an old book or film can bring back floods of memories. For them the pages that follow will provoke unashamed nostalgia. For others, curious about the past, the trivia, the minor happenings, the names on the cigarette packets, the books that created a stir, they will vividly convey the atmosphere of life as it was lived between the wars.

Twopenny Libraries, Crosswords and Penguins

IT WAS the day of the 7s 6d novel. Vera Brittain's autobiography *Testament of Youth* cost 8s 6d when it appeared in 1933, while Eric Partridge's *Slang Today and Yesterday* was yours for 21s—all 486 pages of it. Even so, the bookshop was uninviting; as the Chief Librarian of Boot's Booklovers Library between the wars summed it up, many people 'would hesitate to enter one of the better-class bookshops or libraries because they would feel mentally and socially ill at ease in its unaccustomed atmosphere'.

The National Book Council (ancestor of today's National Book League) in a report on the Sunday Times Book Exhibition of 1934 lamented that the 'great majority of the visitors to the Exhibition have been described as Class A circulating library subscribers. Generally speaking they were well-to-do people, mostly women.' And no wonder. The exhibition was held in 1933 at Sunderland House, Curzon Street, and in 1934 at Grosvenor House, Park Lane. It opened at the ladylike hour of 11 o'clock in the morning and remained open for an hour or so after work. It was an era when people still knew their place and Mayfair was not the place for the majority.

Yet for the educated upper class, it wasn't 'done' to attend a dinner party or social function without being reasonably well briefed about the latest books; and with maids, cooks and nannies, there was time for this to be done. It was after World War II that the conversation revolved around domestic troubles rather than troubles with domestics.

Each Sunday the 'heavies' devoted at least twelve pages to book reviews. The publishers' advertisements—11in double columns or larger—announced their publications loud and clear. Gollancz set the pace with clear bold typography, dominating the book pages of the *Observer* and leaving his competitors to shout it out amongst themselves in what space was left to them. *The Observer, Sunday Times, Daily Telegraph* and—until 1937—the *Morning Post* were influential, with names such as J. L. Garvin, Desmond MacCarthy, Sir John Squire, Ralph Strauss and Harold Nicolson; while every Thursday in the *Evening Standard*, Arnold Bennett's pen could guarantee a second

The 1930s when there was space for book reviews and literary giants to do the reviewing. Publishers announced their titles with panache. At least Gollancz did

edition overnight.

Sales of books were still aimed at, and largely confined to, the upper classes. The Times, Mudies, Harrods, with their 'guaranteed' subscriptions, could produce any new book on demand. Harrods' annual 'guaranteed' subscription in 1935 was £5 9s 6d for three volumes. Lower down the social scale the public library was in constant use and its importance as an educational medium was increasing; but there were those in the upper echelons of society who scorned to go there. To use it was the equivalent (in those days) of sending one's children to state schools. Apart from the fact that the latest books were not available on demand, the books themselves must, by nature of the users, be contaminated. Thomas Joy records that wealthy lady subscribers to Harrods' library would pay extra 'to borrow each time absolutely new books, because they were afraid of contamination from a book which had been in other hands'.

Those who found The Times, Mudies and Harrods too expensive obtained their library books from W. H. Smith and Boots, each firm offering different subscription categories depending on a book's availability. In the 1930s, Boots bought over a million books a year. W. H. Smith had three categories of library service. 'Preferential', at an annual subscription of £1 15s, supplied the subscriber with one book at a time of any title demanded. 'Class A' made available, for £1 a year, the most up-to-date books, although you might have to wait your turn. 'Class B' included all but the latest books for an annual subscription of 10s, although if you were not content with one book at a time, but needed three, you would have to find another 5s. W. H. Smith also sold books, and announced in the *Times Literary Supplement*

W. H. Smith Library. Place unknown, time forgotten

A best seller but Sorrell, as depicted on the wrapper, has five fingers on his right hand. It was not discovered until some years after publication

during the late 1920s in an oft-repeated advertisement: 'You can obtain any of the Books advertised or reviewed in "The Times Literary Supplement" through any branch of W. H. Smith & Son.' The great advantage was being able to change a library book at any branch. Nothing was more pleasant, on a seaside holiday, than to walk into a Boots or W. H. Smith library in the High Street. The sun always seemed to be shining outside, and with luck one might come away with Warwick Deeping's *Sorrell and Son* or Priestley's *The Good Companions*. Next stop was a deck-chair for half-an-hour's quiet read before lunch, undisturbed by a band playing on the distant pier and the shouts of children from the sands below.

Even more popular was the 'no deposit' two-penny library. In every town and village up and down the country, the small stationer and tobacconist opened a twopenny library, gener-

ally renting from a wholesale library stock which was changed periodically. The twopenny library was a challenge to the public library which made little attempt at that time to cater for the reader who wanted the latest novel. The demand was for what was termed in those days as 'slush'. Nat Gould's racing novels in which the winner took all, and the cloak-and-dagger mysteries of William Le Queux were eagerly read. The sinister Dr Fu Manchu, yellow and mysterious, sent welcome shudders down the spine, while swinging from tree to tree was Tarzan, the creation of Edgar Rice Burroughs. The romantically-inclined could indulge their palpitating hearts with *The Sheik of Araby*.

The books reflect the changing moods of life in Britain. In the first five years after the war, the fears of readjustment after a long period of hardship and shortages, life was apparently going to be fun and daring, and the books read

(*left*) *Arnold Bennett with the actress Lilah McCarthy at a ball at Devonshire House in the early twenties.* (*right*) *A. A. Milne.* When We Were Very Young *first published on 6 November 1924 had reached its sixteenth edition by 1927*

at the time catch that mood. Bertie Wooster was introduced by P. G. Wodehouse in *My Man Jeeves*, and the sophisticated daring of Michael Arlen's *The Green Hat* made it a best seller. Somerset Maugham's *The Moon and Sixpence*, Arnold Bennett's *Riceyman Steps*, E. M. Forster's *A Passage to India*, Aldous Huxley's *Crome Yellow*, and A. S. M. Hutchinson's *If Winter Comes* ('Can Spring Be Far Behind?' quoted the second line of the song that followed the popularity of the book) were some of the fiction titles that filled subscribers' lists at the circulating libraries. In 1922 John Galsworthy's *The Forsyte Saga* was already looking back at an age which had vanished. David Garnett's strange novel *Lady into Fox* made a stir in literary circles. Mary Webb's *Precious Bane* remained in comparative obscurity until Stanley Baldwin 'discovered' it some years later. Sapper's *Bulldog Drummond* gave us, in 1920, all the thrills we were seeking; as yet the realistic war novel had not appeared, R. H. Mottram's *The Spanish Farm*, with a preface by John Galsworthy, was not about the horrors of the battlefield, but the effect of war on two young people of different nationality.

T. S. Eliot's *The Waste Land*, symbolic of the immediate post-war era appeared in 1922, and in that same year *Ulysses* by James Joyce, banned in Britain, was published in Paris. (A cartoon appeared in the *New Yorker* showing a middle-aged American matron hesitatingly inquiring of a man behind a left-bank bookstall '*Avez-vous Ulysses?*') The strictly European view of culture and art was being challenged, and H. G. Wells in his *Outline of History* attempted to describe the wider horizons of world history. We welcomed Christopher Robin, immortalised by A. A. Milne, and his illustrator Ernest Shepherd in *When We Were Very Young*.

Between 1926 and 1930 the high hopes of the immediate post-war period were beginning to look jaded. The gay 'wild' life was on the way out and reading took a more serious turn. However, there was time to laugh at Anita Loos' *Gentlemen Prefer Blondes*, and the two Evelyn Waugh novels, *Decline and Fall* and *Vile Bodies*. In 1926 from America came Theodore Dreiser's massive *The American Tragedy*, and from Germany the equally impressive *Jew Süss* by Lion Feuchtwanger. Elinor Glyn's *It* was naughty but nice. For complete contrast there was Bernard Shaw's *An Intelligent Woman's Guide to Socialism*, published two years later. Somerset Maugham's *Ashenden*,

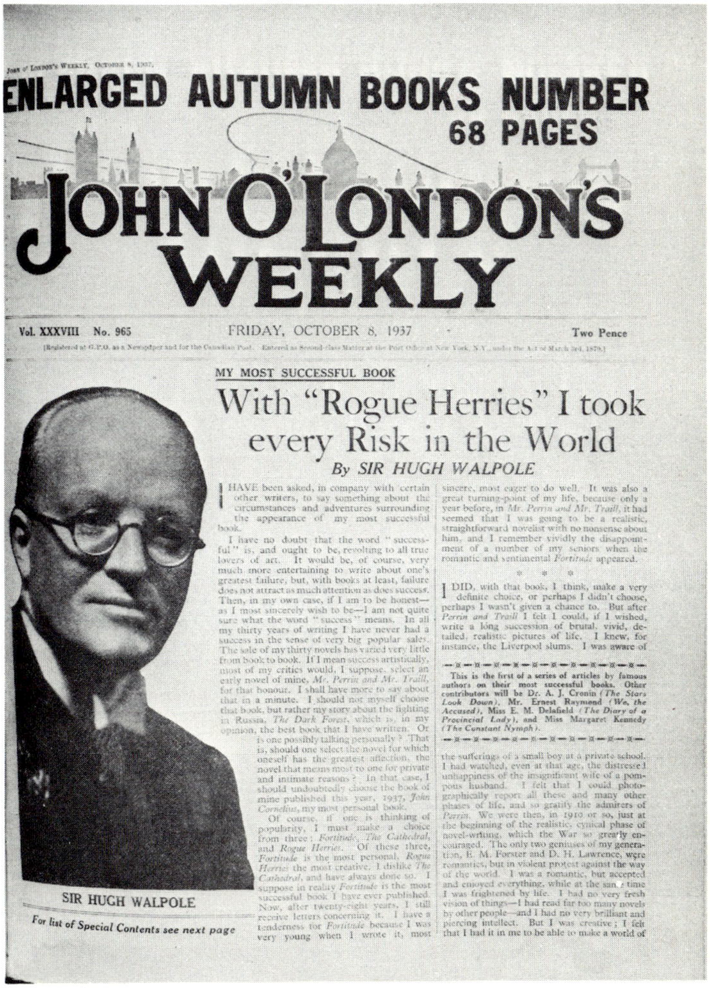

ENLARGED AUTUMN BOOKS NUMBER
68 PAGES

JOHN O'LONDON'S WEEKLY

Vol. XXXVIII No. 965 FRIDAY, OCTOBER 8, 1937 Two Pence

MY MOST SUCCESSFUL BOOK

With "Rogue Herries" I took every Risk in the World

By SIR HUGH WALPOLE

I HAVE been asked, in company with certain other writers, to say something about the circumstances and adventures surrounding the appearance of my most successful book.

I have no doubt that the word "successful" is, and ought to be, revolting to all true lovers of art. It would be, of course, very much more entertaining to write about one's greatest failure, but, with books at least, failure does not attract as much attention as does success. Then, in my own case, if I am to be honest—as I most sincerely wish to be—I am not quite sure what the word "success" means. In all my thirty years of writing I have never had a success in the sense of very big popular sales. The sale of my thirty novels has varied very little from book to book. If I mean success artistically, most of my critics would, I suppose, select an early novel of mine, *Mr. Perrin and Mr. Traill*, for that honour. I shall have more to say about that in a minute. I should not myself choose that book, but rather my story about the fighting in Russia, *The Dark Forest*, which is, in my opinion, the best book that I have written. Or is one possibly talking personally? That is, should one select the novel for which oneself has the greatest affection, the novel that means most to one for private and intimate reasons? In that case, I should undoubtedly choose the book of mine published this year, 1937, *John Cornelius*, my most personal book.

Of course, if one is thinking of popularity, I must make a choice from three: *Fortitude*, *The Cathedral*, and *Rogue Herries*. Of these three, *Fortitude* is the most personal, *Rogue Herries* the most creative. I dislike *The Cathedral*, and have always done so. I suppose in reality *Fortitude* is the most successful book I have ever published. Now, after twenty-eight years, I still receive letters concerning it. I have a tenderness for *Fortitude* because I was very young when I wrote it, most sincere, most eager to do well. It was also a great turning-point of my life, because only a year before, in *Mr. Perrin and Mr. Traill*, it had seemed that I was going to be a realistic, straightforward novelist with no nonsense about him, and I remember vividly the disappointment of a number of my seniors when the romantic and sentimental *Fortitude* appeared.

* * *

I DID, with that book, I think, make a very definite choice, or perhaps I didn't choose, perhaps I wasn't given a chance to. But after *Perrin and Traill* I felt I could, if I wished, write a long succession of brutal, vivid, detailed, realistic pictures of life. I knew, for instance, the Liverpool slums. I was aware of the sufferings of a small boy at a private school. I had watched, even at that age, the distressed unhappiness of the insignificant wife of a pompous husband. I felt that I could photographically report all these and many other phases of life, and so gratify the admirers of *Perrin*. We were then, in 1910 or so, just at the beginning of the realistic, cynical phase of novel-writing, which the War so greatly encouraged. The only two geniuses of my generation, E. M. Forster and D. H. Lawrence, were romantics, but in violent protest against the way of the world. I was a romantic, but accepted and enjoyed everything, while at the same time I was frightened by life. I had no very fresh vision of things—I had read far too many novels by other people—and I had no very brilliant and piercing intellect. But I was creative; I felt that I had it in me to be able to make a world of

This is the first of a series of articles by famous authors on their most successful books. Other contributors will be Dr. A. J. Cronin (*The Stars Look Down*), Mr. Ernest Raymond (*We, the Accused*), Miss E. M. Delafield (*The Diary of a Provincial Lady*), and Miss Margaret Kennedy (*The Constant Nymph*).

SIR HUGH WALPOLE

For list of Special Contents see next page

Sixty-eight pages for twopence—full of news about books!

the hero of espionage, and Thornton Wilder's haunting novel *The Bridge of San Luis Rey*, also appeared during this period. Virginia Woolf's *To the Lighthouse*, and Victoria Sackville-West's *The Edwardians* were two novels likely to be found on the lists of subscribers to Harrods or the Times libraries; but *The Water Gypsies* by A. P. Herbert had a universal appeal. The saga of the Whiteoaks family was launched by Mazo de la Roche; and Hugh Walpole's *Rogue Herries* was the first of the Herries chronicles. Circus life was the subject of Lady Eleanor Smith's *Red Wagon*; and the splendidly teutonic *Grand Hotel* by Vicki Baum revealed the intrigues and romances that occur against the seemingly efficient and unhurried background of a luxury hotel.

This was the period of the war book. T. E. Lawrence's *Revolt in the Desert* was published in 1926; it was an abridgement of *The Seven Pillars of Wisdom* privately published the year before. *Memoirs of a Fox Hunting Man* by Siegfried Sassoon was published in 1928, and the year after, the German view of the horrors of the battlefield was described by Erich Maria Remarque in *All Quiet On The Western Front*. The sales throughout the world amounted to millions. Ernest Hemingway's *A Farewell to Arms*, an explosive story set in wartime Italy with an American soldier and an English nurse as the main characters; Robert Graves' autobiographical *Goodbye To All That*; and Richard Aldington's *Death of a Hero*, were all published in 1929, an eventful year for war books.

Axel Munthe's *The Story of San Michele* was another big seller. The story was fascinating, despite any doubts about how much of it was fiction and how much fact. D. H. Law-

James Barrie with a stick under his arm, takes refreshment in the early hours of the morning at the Charing Cross Coffee stall in 1921

rence's *Lady Chatterley's Lover* was published privately in Italy and Radcliffe Hall's *The Well of Loneliness*, a novel of homosexual female love, was banned after a court case. 'It is the first English novel,' wrote Havelock Ellis in a commentary to the book, 'which presents, in a completely faithful and uncompromising term, one particular aspect of sexual life as it exists among us today.' The 'today' was 1928, but the subject-matter was still unacceptable.

The first half of the thirties was over-shadowed by the Depression: the second by the threat of war. The books of the period contain an awareness of the lives of the underprivileged, and warnings of the dangers of fascism. Walter Greenwood captured the hopelessness of the unemployed in *Love on the Dole*; and Christopher Isherwood's *Mr Norris Changes Trains* had the seamy world of Hitler's Berlin as its setting. Louis Golding's great novel of life in the East End of London, *Magnolia Street*; A. J. Cronin's *Hatter's Castle* with a Scottish background and later, his even more popular *The Stars Look Down*; Eric Linklater's *Juan in America*, were all in great demand. A. G. Street introduced an increasingly urban population to the delights of country life in his *Farmer's Glory*, which he called 'a pen picture of farming life in Southern England and Western Canada', and Stella Gibbons' hilarious take-off of the spud and swede brigade, *Cold Comfort Farm*, had the town-dweller in fits of laughter. Even the countryman had to smile.

Charles Morgan's novel *The Fountain*, essential reading for the literary set, Harvey Allen's *Anthony Adverse* from America, Frances Brett Young's *My Brother Jonathan*, very much from Britain, and the tough *The Postman Always Rings Twice* by J. M. Cain, again from America, were all good sellers in a period of high sales. Virginia Woolf's biography *Flush*, the dog that curled at Elizabeth Barrett Browning's feet, and Victoria Sackville-West's *All Passion Spent*, were published in 1931. Aldous Huxley's *Brave New World* envisaged a new society of humans, and H. G. Wells explained *The Shape of Things To Come*.

Beverley Nichols who had hitherto guided us up and down various garden paths wrote a controversial book *Cry Havoc!* about the futility of war and preparing for it. Pacifist beliefs were widely held at the time. In the same year A. G. Macdonnell's *England, Their England* appeared. Who could forget the hilarious description of the cricket match?

From 1936 to the outbreak of war, books predicting the horrors to come were greedily devoured. Facts that were known to be true, but found unacceptable, were confirmed by John Gunther in *Inside Europe* and by Douglas Reed

A Foyle's Literary Luncheon held in January, 1935. The Rev 'Dick' Sheppard speaking here. Other speakers were James Maxton, Lord Raglan, St John Ervine, Marie Stopes and Basil Dean. Cecil Roberts presided and the theme was 'If I were Dictator', a topical subject at that time

in *Insanity Fair*. George Orwell, writing from the depth of his being, gave a picture in *The Road to Wigan Pier* of a grim England very remote from the comfortable, pleasure-seeking existence of the reading public.

When not reading about the horrors that seemed inevitable, you could bury yourself in Margaret Mitchell's *Gone With The Wind*, Winifred Holtby's Yorkshire *South Riding* and Daphne du Maurier's Cornish *Rebecca*. At a more esoteric level there was Charles Morgan's *Sparkenbroke* and Virginia Woolf's *The Years*. T. H. White had an immense following after his *The Sword and the Stone* was published, a book he dedicated to the fifteenth-century knight Sir Thomas Maleore.

Ulysses could now be read; it had been published in England in 1936. Lancelot Hogben's *Mathematics for the Million*, 'a popular self educator' written by the author for fun during a long illness, captured the attention of thousands of mathematically minded readers and was a bestseller. Richard Llewellyn's *How Green Was My Valley* published one month before war broke out, had Wales for its setting. Graham Greene's *Brighton Rock* with its riveting opening sentence, 'Hale knew they meant to murder him before he had been in Brighton three hours', was published in 1938.

The above can only be a selection of between-the-wars books. For there will be readers whose favourite authors were Dorothy Sayers, Edgar Wallace and Agatha Christie—it was the great period of the detective novel. There will be some whose history was permanently coloured by *1066 and All That*. Nevertheless, it gives a cross-section of titles and authors. It is interesting to pick out those that are read with enjoyment today, some forty years later.

Authors at that time were remote from their readers. Their image was not 'projected' to the masses, as the means of projection were limited. This had advantages. Readers looked upon authors with a certain amount of awe, and the authors, remote in their ivory towers, had a vested interest in keeping things that way. Today every detail of authors' lives can be known by their readers, who have thus discovered that they are the most ordinary of mortals, only occasionally living up to expectations, but rarely exceeding them.

Miss Christina Foyle took an important step

Auden, Day Lewis and Spender. Influential between-the-wars. This photograph was taken in 1949

in bringing author and reader together when, on 21 October 1930, she initiated the first Foyle's Literary Lunch. It was held at the Holborn Restaurant (now no more) with Sir Gerald du Maurier in the chair, and Lord Justice Darling, who had just published a book of poems, speaking on 'Inelegant Literature'. The lunch cost 5s a head. Later the event took place in grander surroundings—Grosvenor House, Park Lane—and a particular book and author were always promoted. The audience consisted for the most part of women—in, one recollects, a variety of magnificent hats. If husbands could spare the time, they were of course welcome. The speeches were often amusing and the author was available to sign copies of his or her book. The *Tatler* and *Bystander* of the day reported it as a social event and as the price of the meal increased to an outrageous 7s 6d in the late 1930s, so did the popularity of the occasion.

It was not until 30 July 1935 that the problem of bringing books to the masses took a step forward. In the bookshops there appeared ten new paperback books. The covers were arresting—bold orange, blue and green, each decorated with a black-and-white penguin. The first titles included novels, thrillers, biographies, and among the authors were Ernest Hemingway, André Maurois, Compton Mackenzie, Dorothy Sayers and Agatha Christie. Although attempts had previously been made by other publishers to launch paperbacks, Penguins achieved the breakthrough. At 6d each, books by authors not necessarily considered 'popular'

The first cross-word puzzle published in Britain in 1924

CROSS-WORD PUZZLE COMPETITION.

SOMETHING NEW IN PROBLEMS.

TEN PRIZES FOR CORRECT SOLUTIONS.

CROSS WORD PUZZLES! Here is the great new pastime which it may be predicted with confidence will be the rage of England as soon as it becomes known.

It is a puzzle which any one can solve with the aid of perseverance, ingenuity, and, possibly, a dictionary.

The "Sunday Express," in introducing the Cross Word Puzzle to England, is starting a novel amusement for people of all ages that is certain to become a craze.

What is a Cross-Word Puzzle? Look at the accompanying example. You will see a rectangular figure divided into sixteen small squares, of which four are black. Only the white squares concern you. They are not numbered consecutively; the numbers indicate the beginning of a word, reading either horizontally or vertically (across or down) the puzzle.

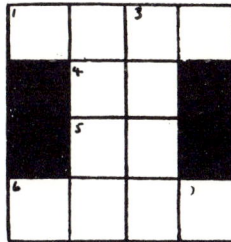

"SUNDAY EXPRESS" CROSS-WORD PUZZLE. NO. 1.

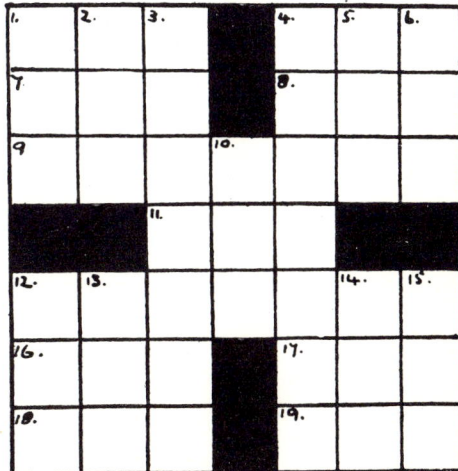

HORIZONTALS.
1. A coin (slang).
4. A tree.
7. Period.
8. Through.
9. Counters of votes.
11. Cosy little room.
12. Drainages.
16. Meaning three (prefix).
17. Snake-like fish.
18. An Oriental coin.
19. Parched.

VERTICALS.
1. Wager.
2. Mineral substance.
3. Eminent political figure.
4. Inflicted retribution.
5. A title.
6. Possesses.
10. Grassland.
12. Home of a certain animal.
13. Before (poetic form).
14. Always (poetic form).
15. Cunning.

All the words used in these problems are to be found in any standard dictionary. Any names that are introduced are those of well-known persons or places.

The "Sunday Express" offers ten prizes of £1 1s. each for correct solutions. Solutions, which must come through the post, must be addressed to :—

The Competition Editor,
"Sunday Express,"
8, Shoe-lane, Fleet-street, E.C.4.

No letters will be opened before 11 a.m. on Tuesday, November 4, when they will be taken at random from the mailbags. The prizes will be awarded to the first ten correct solutions thus opened. The Editor's decision is final.

Now read the following definition :—
HORIZONTALS.
1. At that time.
4. Place where.
5. Behold.
6. Measures of weight.

VERTICALS.
2. Circle of light.
3. A famous school.

Try No. 1. At that time . . . is it "Then"? Fill it in along the top line. No. 2, vertical, must begin with H, which already fills that space. Obviously "Halo." No. 3, vertical, a public school beginning with E—"Eton." Nos. 4 and 5 have automatically completed themselves; "measures of weight," with O.N. in the middle, must be " Tons."

This is, of course, a very easy example, but it shows the system by which Cross Word Puzzles are solved. Horizontals and verticals combine to form words which interlock, and so complete the problem. One incorrect word will prevent this.

Having mastered the method, try your hand at the first "Sunday Express" Cross Word which follows. This, too, is comparatively simple of solution. Next week's problem will be more difficult.

CROSS-WORD PUZZLE—No. 1.

43

THE CROSS-WORD MANIA.

Doctor (rung up at 2 a.m.) "YES, DR. BROWN SPEAKING. WHAT IS IT?"
Voice. "I WANT THE NAME OF A BODILY DISORDER OF SEVEN LETTERS, OF WHICH THE SECOND LETTER MUST BE 'N.'"

From Punch, *July 1925*

44

were within the reach of those who would not have bought at a higher price. The forbidding bookshops stocked them, but, more important, they could also be purchased on the station platform and at the local chain store. Pelicans and Puffins followed. Titles of specialised interest appeared, embracing a cross-section of literature which, it was thought at the time, would never sell in the necessary quantities. Against opposition from almost everyone in the book trade, the late Allen Lane went ahead. A revolution in reading had occurred.

Almost one year later another publishing venture, one which was to have political repercussions after World War II, was launched. The Left Book Club was founded in May 1936 as a result of the political awakening of thousands who had suffered from the economic troubles and depression of the post-war years. Victor Gollancz, a publisher already known for the unconventional and individual way in which he promoted his books, founded the Left Book Club with the object of producing books at popular prices dealing with the dangers of fascism, the threat of war and the existence of poverty. He wanted to warn people against the dangers confronting them. While the political parties floundered, the Left Book Club fearlessly exposed the shortcomings and blatant apathy of the nation's leaders. The books did not mince words. Straight-from-the-shoulder in content and expression, it was 'the most successful political adventure of our generation' wrote Gollancz. By 1939 there were 57,000 registered members and 1,500 Left Discussion Groups. The Left Book Club did not save Britain from war, but it undoubtedly changed people's attitudes towards it, and the political thinking that resulted was an important influence in the return of the Labour Party to power in 1945.

There were diversions other than books to relieve the mind of the pressing problems of the day. The crossword craze began in 1924—the first appearing in the *Sunday Express*—and gained such momentum that even *The Times* succumbed after numerous requests from its readers. A crossword puzzle had been running in the weekly edition, but on 1 February 1930 one appeared on page 7 of *The Times* itself. 'I am a young woman,' wrote a reader, 'but I hate to see a great newspaper pandering to the modern craze for passing the time in all kinds of stupid ways.' It was a cry in the wilderness. On 1 March a Latin crossword appeared and a 'fourth leader' to go with it. The New York *Evening Post* published *The Times* Crossword No 1 and revealed that an enthusiastic crossword solver had taken one and a quarter hours, whereas he generally polished off the *Evening Post* crossword in seven minutes. Quite what that did for Anglo-American relations is not revealed.

It became a feature of most journals to publish a crossword puzzle suitable for their readers' mentality. Puzzles took different shapes and forms—anything for variety—and the relative merits of clues became a topic of extreme boredom. One-upmanship in speed of solving became of foremost importance. People turned first to the solution to yesterday's crossword. The news could wait. War clouds might gather, the economy could be in danger, but what really mattered was that six across should be correct, and that old Boggins sitting opposite should get it wrong.

When it came to a war, China was remote, but games were different and Mah-Jong, originating in China, reached Britain via America. The sets were expensive, books of instruction were numerous and people sat around the table behind their 'walls' of domino-like tiles triumphantly calling 'Pung for a pair Mah-Jong', or talking with a suitable air of oriental mystery about 'Winds' and 'Dragons'. We also played Monopoly. We built houses and hotels on Mayfair and Park Lane, scorned the squalor of the Old Kent Road where the rents were miserably low, Went to Jail, Took a Chance, Paid Income Tax and kept the paper money amounting to thousands close to our chests.

It was all a game, then.

Crystal Sets and the Cat's Whisker

HUDDLED in a chair at the corner of a table, headphones fixed firmly over the ears, a faraway expression on the face, the right hand manipulated the cat's whisker on to the crystal. Others in the room, sensing they were missing something—and indeed they were—offered unwelcome help and advice. With a free hand they were waved away. This was your own private world. At last the crystal 'responded'. By trial and error the whisker had been manipulated on to the sensitive crystal, and after a preliminary crackle, music or speech could be heard. Triumphantly, you leaned back in your chair with a smug smile on your face. Then some careless idiot would jog the table, the cat's whisker shifted and—silence. Removing the headphones you spoke your mind in no uncertain way. You then resumed the struggle until the cat's whisker resumed its rightful place on the crystal once more.

Listening-in was an adventure. In order to achieve satisfactory reception, considerable skill was required. Crystal sets were cheap at 7s 6d, with headphones costing 2s and an aerial 1s 8d. The crystal set in a matchbox was a popular seller but, even when it was superseded by the more sophisticated valve set, listening was not without difficulties.

A comment from Punch, *1926*

Husband (to listening-in Wife). "WHAT'S THE MATTER, DEAR? IS IT BAD NEWS OR STRAVINSKY?"

It was fun building your own set. Journals such as *Wireless Constructor* were a feast of diagrams and instructions. There were an infinite variety of sets that could be constructed; and although valve-holders, rheostats, terminals and the like were identical in all sets, the key to good reception lay in how they were wired up. In the 1920s it was, in America, more expensive to construct a set than to buy one, although that was not the case in Britain. Nothing, though, would take away the appeal of doing your own thing. For the non-constructive types there were valve sets to buy. A four-valve cabinet receiver at £49 8s, with a multitude of accessories, would have a solid cabinet, incorporating the loudspeaker concealed by doors that opened and closed. By 1926 a portable radio receiver was available.

You were rarely satisfied with the reception from a radio set. 'Don't forget' warned the British Broadcasting Company, 'that when you oscillate you are running the risk of having your licence cancelled by the Post-master General.' Oscillate or not, the thrill of getting a foreign station was tremendous. The times when you swore you had got Barcelona—the music was so Spanish—but the voice at the end so very 2LO. With the BBC Handbook by your side you could travel to foreign parts. Berlin—'*Achtung! Hier die Rundfunksender Berlin, auf Wellen . . .*'—with its closing down to the national anthem '*Deutschland über alles*', which the handbook reminded us was 'an old Austrian hymn'. The loudspeaker could be a menace. Its earsplitting crackles, wheezes and screeches disturbed neighbours; but the enthusiastic station-finder remained oblivious to the disturbance his knob-twiddling caused.

The British Broadcasting Company was formed in 1922 and stations were set up in London (2LO), Birmingham (5IT), Manchester (2YZ) and later at Newcastle, Cardiff, Glasgow, Aberdeen and Bournemouth. The news bulletins, read in London, were broadcast simultaneously from all stations. Children's hour was at five o'clock daily with its retinue of favourite 'aunts' and 'uncles'. In 1926 Sir

In 1923 wireless in the dining car of the London–Liverpool express was something of a novelty. London was received fifty miles out, and later the set was tuned in to Birmingham

'Gert and Daisy'—Elsie and Doris Waters. Their cross-talk had wireless listeners in fits of laughter. They showed us as we really were

Walford Davies broadcast to schools and a horn loudspeaker relayed the message to attentive classes. A. J. Alan, the story-teller, whose approach to broadcasting was to convey his personality and not just his voice had a great following; and John Henry must have been the first radio comedian of national fame. 'Good evening, England, this is Gillie Potter speaking to you in basic English' was an opening that had listeners happy in anticipation. There was the one-time schoolmaster who gave up teaching and became Stainless Stephen while later, in 1938, Arthur Askey and Richard 'Stinker' Murdoch in *Band Waggon* was a weekly date that meant no engagements away from home.

It was not until 1927 that commentaries on sporting events were freed from the restrictive practices initiated by newspaper interests. The press guarded its right to describe events and reveal winners. It was possible to listen to the horses' hooves thundering round Tattenham Corner in the rain—you might also hear the rain—but no description could be broadcast and nor could the winner be revealed.

When the restriction was lifted, sporting commentaries reached a wide audience, and it was not considered strange that a sporting event should be 'heard' and not 'seen'. Racing enthusiasts will remember the vivid descriptions of Meyrick Good and Geoffrey Gilbey. The excitement of association and rugby football was conveyed respectively by George Allison and H. B. T. Wakelam. In the *Radio Times* there appeared a plan of the field divided into squares A, B, C etc, and above the voice of the commentator, another voice revealed in which square the ball was being played.

Sir Walford Davies gave many people a

'Ridgeway Parade'—the wireless revue. Philip Ridgeway rehearses the 'opening chorus' in 1930

Broadcasting Shakespeare at Marconi House in 1923

better understanding and appreciation of music. E. M. Stephen's French lessons were not only instructive but entertaining. Marion Cran's talks on gardening fell on receptive ears and her advice was followed by thousands of enthusiastic gardeners. In a Surrey wood in 1924 Miss Beatrice Harrison, playing her 'cello, struck a responsive chord in the elusive nightingale. This famous recording was heard in the comfort of homes all over the country; there was no need to indulge in any spartan fieldwork. In 1923 a debate was broadcast—'that communism would be a danger to the good of the people'—a daring subject for the time. In the same year, a series of talks for women was initiated which developed into *Woman's Hour*.

More and more people liked to be entertained in their own homes. Norman Long ('a song, a smile and a piano'), Clapham and Dwyer, Flotsam and Jetsam, Layton and Johnstone—

Christopher Stone's considered comments on the gramophone records of the day created as much interest as today's fast-talking disc jockeys

(*above*) *Lew Stone, the famous dance band leader, in a BBC Recording Studio, 1934.*

(*below*) *Baird television in pre-BBC days! December 1928 was the first occasion that a play showing more than one person at a time had ever been broadcast. Below is a scene from John Maddison Morton's one-act play 'Box and Cox' first performed at the Royal Lyceum Theatre some eighty years before*

there was a fund of light entertainment to be enjoyed. Tommy Handley—a member of the Roosters' Concert Party—was known in 1926 but became really famous during the war. Reginald Foort played the tunes you liked best on the organ, and Christopher Stone commented on the current gramophone records.

Radio drama developed from being adaptations of stage plays to being specially written for the medium. In 1927 the BBC took over the Promenade Concerts which were in danger of being discontinued. From then the BBC's influence in the world of music increased. The formation of the BBC Symphony Orchestra of 114 players, conducted by Adrian Boult, was followed by the formation of other orchestras such as the theatre orchestra and the light orchestra. Jack ('Say It With Music') Payne was appointed to lead the BBC Dance Orchestra, and from the sophisticated Savoy Hotel came dance music from the Savoy Orpheans to satisfy the craze for jazz and dancing in the late twenties. In countless homes the carpet was rolled back, the sound turned up and young people danced the night away. At the piano might be Carol Gibbons who, with consummate skill, would lead from one tune into the next. One could hardly keep one's feet still. How dull it seemed after the close down!

Broadcasting reflected all aspects of life. Its impact was considerable and in moments of crisis (such as the General Strike of 1926) it was a steadying influence. Literature, drama, music—even politics—became less remote.

'Felix Kept on Walking' and 'If I had a Talking Picture of You'

'100 PER CENT ALL TALKING PICTURES . . . ALL SINGING . . . ALL TALKING . . . ALL DANCING' read the brash signs behind the eager queues outside the cinemas in the early thirties. The ear-drum splitting era had arrived. For before the talkies there was only the pianist in the corner by the screen playing his (or her) way through a film, skilfully matching the tempo and mood to the action of the film. The film itself flickered; the actors movements were jerky and exaggerated. The sub-titles flashed on the screen to tell us what was being said and done, and depending on our reading speed, we complained that they lingered too long and held up the action of the film, or vanished before we had reached the vital last words. But what words were needed to explain the meaning of a twitch of Charlie Chaplin's moustache, or the raising of his eyebrow? Charlie, holding Jackie Coogan's hand as they shuffled off down a street in *The Kid* conveyed the loneliness and sadness without resource to sub-titles. Only the piano changed its tune. Buster Keaton, Harold Lloyd, Fatty Arbuckle, Laurel and Hardy had us rolling in the aisles; Tom Mix in a Western, Douglas Fairbanks in *The Thief of Baghdad* had us riveted to our seats—or benches, more likely.

Many cinemas were flea-pits—small, cramped and hot—a breeding ground for infectious complaints such as measles and chicken-pox from which well-brought-up children from 'nice' homes must be protected. A sickly sweet smell of oranges and human sweat invaded the nostrils, but it was all wonderful. There was the serial film with the heroine, lashed with ropes to the railway line, awaiting inevitable death from the fast approaching train. Nearer and nearer it came—nothing could stop it surely? CONTINUED NEXT WEEK! And back we went, week after week after week. Pearl White was often the damsel in distress. Lon Chaney had so many disguises—remember *The Hunchback of Notre Dame*?—that it needed some adjustment to move from the make-believe of the screen to the reality of everyday life. Surely the old tramp on the other side of the road might be Chaney in yet another disguise? Rin Tin Tin bounding through adventure after adventure and coming out Top Dog; later Felix, the animated cartoon feline, who kept on walking, kept on walking, kept on walking into every explosive trouble, and into the hearts of his thousands of followers of all ages. Felix was the forerunner of other animated animals—Pluto, the endearing long-eared long-legged dog, and Mickey, the resourceful mouse.

Mary Pickford was our sweetheart; Pola Negri the woman we would leave home for. Janet Gaynor and Norma Shearer were such nice girls, and each had a faithful following. And the men! The long eyelashes, the penetrating eyes that reduced the bones to marrow! Ramon Novarro, brave and impetuous in *The Prisoner of Zenda* (1922) or tearing around the arena in a chariot in *Ben Hur* (1926) with a profile only to be bettered (some think) by Rudolph Valentino as he gazed into the eyes of Alice Terry in *The Four Horsemen of the Apocalypse* (1921). The *Squibs* Comedies in 1921 made Betty Balfour the most popular British star.

In 1920 there were 4,000 cinemas in Great Britain and it was estimated that half as many again were required, but in spite of this upsurge of interest in the cinema, the British film industry was going through a series of crises. The American grip on the industry made it impossible for British film producers to get adequate return on the immense sums of money that film-making required.

Through the thirties, Hollywood set the pace. What the stars wore, ate, how they behaved, accounts of their love life, true or imaginary—all this was of the utmost importance to the girls working in shops and factories, or to the maid-of-all-work in some grand house.

Tom Mix, cowboy filmstar of the twenties, arrives at Southampton with his wife, daughter and Tony

Queueing at the old Marble Arch Pavilion in the silent days of 1926. Shops have taken the place of the cinema and the foliage has also disappeared

The screen showed luxury and riches; the grim reality in Britain for so many accentuated the contrast.

The cinema moved from the flea-pit to the luxurious. The first super-cinema in central London was the Tivoli in the Strand built in the early twenties. Between 1924 and 1928, more super cinemas spread across London. The Capitol in the Haymarket (now the Haymarket Odeon), the Astoria in Charing Cross Road and the Regal at Marble Arch (now the Odeon) opened their doors to a public that demanded better presentation of films and more comfort in which to view them. The cinemas were transformed into gaudy buildings of chromium and gilt, with lush carpeting and deep padded seats. The organ—the mighty Wurlitzer—rose phoenix-like from the depths, only to sink back bathed in shimmering coloured lights at the start of the programme.

The arrival of the talkies in 1928 shattered a number of illusions, and careers. Dashing good looks were no compensation for a thin reedy voice. But there could be no going back, for the public loved the new medium. Warner

John Gilbert with his wife Virginia Bruce

53

(*above left*) *Lillian ('Broken Blossoms') Gish. Fair hair, blue eyes, 5ft 4in.*
(*above right*) *Ramon Gil Sameniegos—Ramon Novarro to you—and maybe (at the time) a heart throb to your wife.* (*below left*) *The funmakers. Roscoe ('Fatty') Arbuckle and Buster Keaton.* (*below right*) *Clara Bow, the 'It' Girl. Red hair, brown eyes, 5ft 3½in*

There they are—stars of the silent days with one of the greatest of them all, Mary Pickford, standing by the fireplace. She holds May McAvoy's hand and from her left to right Claire Adams, Edna Murphy, Mildred Davies, Clare Horton, Laura La Plante, Helen Ferguson. Back row from the left: Virginia Fox, Viola Dana Gloria Hope, Gertrude Olmstead, Patsy Ruth Miller and Marjorie Daw

Brothers' first talkie *The Jazz Singer* with Al Jolson, followed by the same star in *The Singing Fool* had every delivery boy whistling the tune featured. 'Sonny Boy' was a particular favourite and it sounded grand in the bath. By 1930 all the large cinemas and most of the small ones were wired for the talkies.

With the talkies arrived a host of new actors and actresses. Not only were people heard to speak; machines were heard to work. Aircraft diving in *Hell's Angels* (1930), the sinister background sound of a train on the rails in *The Lady Vanishes*—a great Hitchcock film with light relief supplied by Naunton Wayne

and Basil Radford. The crack of the rifle and the stampede of horses in Westerns added a vibrant reality that made the tinkling piano (or even the orchestra that replaced it) seem poor and insipid in conveying the exciting drama projected on the screen. It was all for real. The sackings of numerous musicians who had formed cinema orchestras added to the sum total of the unemployed. Ironically it was the film musical that, with the arrival of talkies, became a possibility that was exploited to the full. Majestic sets were created as a background for the new type of star that was emerging— the star who could sing and dance. Fred

55

'Charlie'

Astaire and Ginger Rogers danced their way through *The Gay Divorce* and many other films. Jeanette MacDonald and Maurice Chevalier enchanted thousands in *The Love Parade*. Deanna Durbin in *A Hundred Men and a Girl* was acclaimed as a brilliant discovery; a film which —if launched today with such a title would suggest an 'X' certificate—was of universal appeal. On a more operatic level, Grace Moore in *One Night of Love* made popular the song of that title.

Musicals were noisy and often brash. It was nice, for a change, to hear the hero whisper sweet nothings into the heroine's ear and then, seconds later, the sound of passionate breathing that culminated in the kiss that ended the film. However intimate the scene on the screen, there we sat in the massive chromium-plated cinema, sharing our emotions with hundreds of strangers. The cosy intimacy of the flea-pit was gone, the comforting tinkle of the piano would never return, except as a curiosity. In its place there was strident noise. Everything and everyone in the film world was larger than life. When the show was over we emerged, blinking, into the real world, that seemed so much smaller and quieter.

Felix—the star of 1925—created by Pat Sullivan

'Dancing Time'

'I'M Ceres the Goddess of Plenty, and plenty I've had in my day', sang Douglas Byng appropriately attired at the Café de Paris in Leicester Square. The Café de Paris was one of the many night-spots offering dinner, dancing and cabaret. To reach the dance floor one descended a gracious, curved staircase in full view of the other diners. It was quite an ordeal; it needed concentration to 'make an entry'. It was equally important to make a satisfactory exit and to instil dignity into the rear view while going back up the staircase was even more difficult.

As the diners arrived more tables and chairs were placed on the dance floor, so that the space left for dancing became smaller and smaller. The dancing couples could hardly move. Music was played by Jack Harris and his band. Waiters squeezed between the tables to serve the food; between courses, couples left their tables to dance. Douglas Byng commented that so crowded could it be on occasions, that his red wig was very nearly fried on a hot plate as he passed through the kitchen to the ballroom for his act. It cost all of £5 for two at the Café de Paris and that included dinner, dancing, cabaret, drinks and tip.

The cabaret 'turn' was popular at that time. The atmosphere was intimate and expensive, the audience receptive, well fed and beautifully dressed. (Lounge suits were permitted in the gallery of the Café de Paris, but nothing less than a 'black tie' was acceptable on the dance floor.) Cabaret artistes were special. They needed to be sophisticated and in fashion. They performed only to the wealthy, and frequently moved in the same social circles. Audiences were limited in number and packed into a small area, quite unlike a music hall or theatre, and it needed a certain technique to succeed. Beatrice Lillie was one of the greatest. She would begin a song in semi-serious vein and then, unaccountably her voice might rise or sink an octave and she would look at her audience in pained surprise that they should be laughing so much. Occasionally she wore a long string of pearls which she swung round her neck in ever-increasing circles until the momentum caused her to totter. Layton and Johnstone, the two negro singers, were extremely successful, the former at the piano. The Yacht Club Boys and the Mills Brothers, close-harmony acts, were the type of entertainers that fitted into cabaret so well. Gwen Farrar and Norah Blaney were considered brilliant; Ronald Frankau generally 'blue' but extremely funny. The Savoy, The Berkeley, Grosvenor House were some of the other places to visit, but the real night clubs were altogether different. One 'went on' to a night club after the Café de Paris and Savoy had closed.

Mrs Kate Meyrick was the accepted queen of the night club. She ran the '43' at 43 Gerrard Street, the Silver Slipper with its dance floor of glass in Regent Street, and others. The Licensing Act of 1921 imposed ridiculous restrictions on London's night life. No drinks

Douglas Byng sings 'Spring'

Between-the-wars cabaret artistes:
(*above left*) *The Western Brothers, frightfully good chaps.* (*above right*) '*Hutch*'.
Sentimental songs. (*below left*) *Layton & Johnstone. Close harmony.* (*below right*)
Teddy Brown with xylophone. While playing he would, with amazing agility in
spite of his bulk, turn completely round and resume without missing the sequence
of notes

without food after 11pm and having the glasses removed from the tables after midnight were rules that had to be overcome in some way. In order to circumvent the law, such places became 'clubs' for members only. To become a member presented no great difficulties. The secretary of the 'club' was quite prepared to propose you at first sight, and the commissionaire could be relied upon to act as seconder. The police were unimpressed by the 'club' subterfuge and regularly 'raided' such establishments. The night clubs were frequented by royalty (the Prince of Wales was often to be seen at the Kit-Cat), well-known figures in society, stage and screen stars—embarrassing when a raid took place and those caught breaking the licensing law read like the pages from Debrett. Night clubs were profitable for the proprietors. Champagne at that time cost 12s 6d a bottle but was sold in the night clubs during licensing hours for up to 30s, up to £2 during the 'illegal' hours. So the fines meted out at the magistrates' courts were annoying but not unduly onerous.

The police became tougher and in 1924 Mrs Meyrick was sentenced to six months' imprisonment. Her plight was lamented by her distinguished clientèle, and on her release from Holloway she continued with unbated energy to manage her chain of clubs so that when one was closed by the police, the others could carry on. By 1930 the police had won the battle; London's night life had become a pale shadow. Nevertheless, Mrs Meyrick, who died poor, managed to educate her sons at public schools and her daughters at Roedean, marrying three of them into the peerage.

The night-club era was the twenties, during the aftermath of the war, when troubles were over and to be forgotten and a new way of life heralded. Only the wealthy could afford their prices and it was the same crowd, night after night, in the same club, until suddenly it became unfashionable and they all moved like well-bred sheep to another that for some reason had become the 'in' place. Nevertheless, there was a spontaneous gaiety about them—brittle

and shallow perhaps—and they served as an effective backcloth for good dance bands and brilliant cabaret artistes. It was possible to dance all evening, go on to a night club and dance until dawn when breakfast was served.

The afternoon presented no problems either, with a *thé dansant* available: the Savoy charged you 5s a head to fritter away an afternoon; the Piccadilly Hotel charged a shilling a head less. The Astoria Dance Hall and the Regent Palace at 2s a head were in a different class with a less select clientèle. It is difficult to create a party spirit on cups of tea, daintily cut sandwiches and cream cakes: a *thé dansant* rarely appeared to be a gay occasion. Clothes were formal, women wore hats and the dance band could hardly be expected to respond in such an atmosphere. After the war there were many

Kate Meyrick, the night-club queen, sits as she receives the acclamations of family, friends and clientèle on her release from Holloway in 1924

59

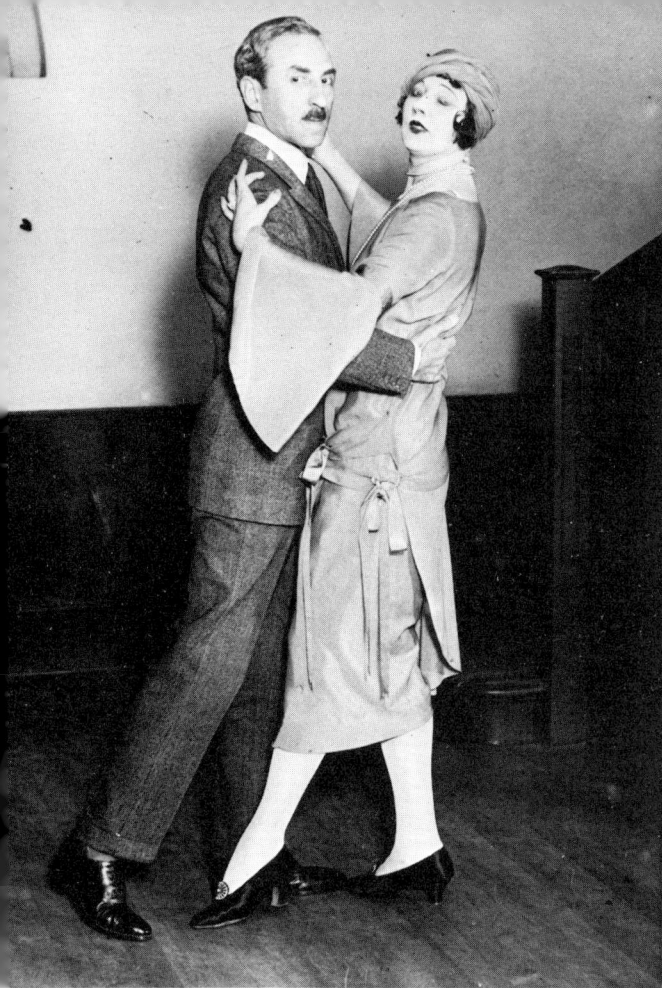

(*left*) *Demonstrating the tango, 1925.* (*right*) *Dancing in full regalia to the gramophone although the word isn't actually mentioned in the advertisement for the Aeolian 'Vocalion'. The year is 1920.*

men who had not returned to work and who had the time to partner their girl-friends, wives or mistresses at a *thé dansant*. Those without partners, often elderly women of uncertain age, employed 'gigolos'. Gigolos, romantic-looking, slim-waisted, elegantly dressed, would for payment partner any lady at a *thé dansant*; they watched in the background for ladies in need of a partner for the afternoon, and possibly on other occasions as well. By the same token, there were 'hostesses' for the lone male, not only at a *thé dansant* but at night clubs too.

'Gigolo' was a term of derision. A father, whose daughter might want to marry someone he considered to be a waster or 'too handsome by half' might refer to the young man as a 'gigolo'.

Dancing in the home could be formal or informal. The latter involved collecting some friends together, supplying light refreshments, rolling back the carpet, putting on the gramophone and dancing until the parents could stand the noise no longer. When the records ran out, switch on the wireless and dance to Carol

THIS DANCE MUST NOT BE PERFORMED IN PUBLIC UNTIL THE EVENING OF 15th NOVEMBER 1938

HOW TO DANCE
The Chestnut Tree

BY
Adele England
Principal: Locarno School of Dancing. 150 Streatham Hill, S.W.

INTRODUCTORY INSTRUCTIONS.

Couples face line of Dance; Gentleman on Lady's left side. Gentleman's right arm is around Lady's waist; Lady's left arm is around Gentleman's waist. Gentleman commences on the left foot: Lady on right foot. The steps described below are for the GENTLEMEN—all Lady's steps commence on the opposite foot. The movement of the "Hop" Step is similar to a Polka hop. The movement of the swing step is performed like the movement of a clock pendulum.

THE HOP STEP four times along the room, counting 1-2-3-Hop. FOUR BARS

THE HALF-CIRCLE.—the Hop Step round the Partners, bringing Lady into Gentleman's position. TWO BARS

Simultaneously with singing the words, 'NEATH THE SPREADING CHESTNUT TREE, perform the actions as follows :

'NEATH
THE
SPREADING
CHEST
NUT
TREE

This takes TWO BARS

NOW,—REPEAT THE WHOLE OF THE ABOVE—EIGHT BARS (Total 16 Bars)

THE SWING STEP. Gentlemen swings right foot forward : Lady swings left foot forward.—Then, Gentleman swings right foot backwards, and Lady swings left foot backwards. REPEAT THE WHOLE OF THIS MOVEMENT. TWO BARS

THE RUN. Take four running steps forward, counting 1-2-3-4. ONE BAR
Then count 5-6, "Stomping" (stamping the feet) at the same time. ONE BAR

NOW—REPEAT THE "SWING STEP" and "THE RUN."—BUT WHEN "STOMPING" SHOUT "CHEST - - NUTS." FOUR BARS
NOW—REPEAT THE "HOP STEP" FOUR TIMES ALONG THE ROOM. FOUR BARS
From now to the end of the dance, the couple remain stationary – the dance being restricted to hand movements only.

Point the index finger (of right hand for Gentleman: of left hand for Lady)—three times, singing "Now you ought to see—"
ONE BAR —"Rest" on fourth beat

The couple bend the knees, and hold one hand outwards from the body (Gentleman left : Lady right)—Count "1." Now raise the hand twice—Count 2-3. "Rest" on fourth beat. ONE BAR
(As you count 1-2-3—sing "The Fam — ily.")

NOW—TO FINISH THE DANCE—REPEAT THE WORDS "NEATH THE SPREADING CHESTNUT TREE" WITH SIMULTANEOUS ACTION. TWO BARS

Gibbons playing at the Savoy. Sometimes there were vocalists; but not with the Savoy Orpheans—just the perfect tempo, tune after tune after tune.

The 'invitation' dance at home was formal. A band was booked—probably piano, sax and drums unless the size of the party demanded something more ambitious—the printed invitations were posted well in advance. Evening dress for the men—generally white tie and tails—was obligatory. At the entrance to the ballroom each guest was handed a dance programme from which dangled a pencil. The men rushed round trying to fill their cards, booking up the most attractive girls, while the plain girls sat nervously by, praying that they would not suffer the embarrassment of being neglected 'wallflowers'. After each dance the gentleman shepherded his partner to a chair and they conversed; perhaps his partner would like some light refreshment—he would go in search of it. When the next dance began, he would politely take his leave and seek out his new partner. The dance immediately before the 'Interval' on the programme was the supper dance and it was important that an attractive partner should be booked for that particular dance. Somebody ugly and dull could ruin an entire evening as supper lasted at least an hour and conversation could—if one was unlucky—be a frightful drag.

Dance steps were the formal fox-trots, waltzes and one-steps. The fox-trot was suitable for small floors, where dancers had more or less to shuffle round, keeping their feet just moving to the music. There was the exotic and arousing tango and, arriving mainly from America, the Shimmy, Charleston and Black-bottom, dances that involved considerable movement of leg and behind, and consequently more floor space. Today, dancers do their own individual thing, but then partners held each other close—almost glued together it was commented—and in the words of the song at that time enjoyed 'dancing cheek to cheek'.

Hammersmith's Palais de Danse opened in 1919 with the Original Dixieland band. In 1923 the great Paul Whiteman arrived in Britain and enthusiasts could see and hear for themselves what had hitherto been a legend. Jack Hylton, Lew Stone and the Savoy Havana Band broadcast regularly and it was bands such as these for which the carpets were rolled back in countless homes. In 1932 the BBC ran a thirty-five minute programme of Duke Ellington and his band, later it made a triumphant tour of Britain. Louis Armstrong and 'Fats' Waller paid a visit in the thirties, and it was then that the soloist, in the form of a hot singer or instrumentalist, was featured. Such interruptions added variety, but often broke the magic of the tempo to which people liked dancing. Names such as Bert Ambrose, Roy Fox, Ray Noble and Jack Jackson recall the days when, in the words of the 1924 song, 'You and I were dancing.'

Making an Exhibition of Ourselves

THE BRITISH Empire Exhibition covered some 220 acres at Wembley and opened in April 1924. It was, in the words of the official catalogue 'designed to display the natural resources of the various countries within the Empire, and the activities, industrial and social, of their peoples'. This was achieved by housing the exhibits in pavilions, solid in structure and unimaginative architecturally, at an estimated cost of £12 million. Amongst 'A Thousand and One Items of Interest' were the Queen's Dolls' House in the Palace of Arts which raised some £20,000 for charity; 'putting THE EYES INTO NEEDLES' at the rate of 250 per minute in the

Royal Tour, Wembley style.
Queen Mary with the Queen of Italy

Miscellaneous Textiles Section of the Palace of Industry; a view of the BIGGEST KNIFE IN THE WORLD containing 1,924 blades ('one for each year of the Christian era'); a full-sized model of the Prince of Wales with horse and typical Canadian Homestead as background' SCULPTURED IN BUTTER (North east corner of Canada); a MOUNTAINOUS PINEAPPLE 20ft high reproduced in metal (South Africa); a WILD BOAR speared by HRH Prince of Wales (Jungle Exhibit, India) and a GIGANTIC CHEESE weighing $\frac{1}{2}$ tons made from 3,000 gallons of milk (Australia).

Visitors to the serious exhibits in the Palaces of Industry and Engineering, and in the Pavilions displaying the prowess of a still-united Empire, could hear the shrieks of excitement from the Amusement Park where the gigantic switchback and other massive stomach-turning thrills (including the Whip which 'can attain a maximum speed of 20 miles per hour') were a magnetic attraction for thousands. On a quieter note there was the Palace of Beauty in which the visitor saw 'living presentments of ten of the most beautiful women known in history' from Cleopatra to Miss 1924. The visitors needed to be fed: the wealthy visited the Lucullus; those with less money, the Grand Restaurant (lunch 5s, tea 2s 6d, dinner 10s 6d). Scattered all over the 220 acres were cafés serving fish (from 6d), tea (at 3d per cup) and half a meat pie for 6d. Unlike the 1851 Exhibition, this one was not 'dry'.

When the Exhibition closed in November, 17 million visitors had footslogged through it. But it lost money. How many remembered ten years from then, giving a cursory glance at the League of Nations Union Kiosk (not Pavilion or Palace), with the illuminated copy of the Articles of the Convenant subscribed to by fifty-four nations, on view?

Just over ten years later—on 6 May 1935—George V's Silver Jubilee was celebrated; a reign of twenty-five years through a period of danger and anguish. Surely now the clouds would roll away? London looked its best. The sun shone; it was 75°F in the shade. The parks had been open the night before, and those lucky enough to find a deck chair paid 2d to sit in it until dawn broke. Others slept on the grass, and everybody behaved. 'There hasn't been a single flower broken in beds, in spite of all the thousands sitting on the grass and having a picnic at night,' commented a park keeper. 'Not a blooming flower, as far as I can see.' The massed colours of the irises and tulips and the flowering hawthorns set a scene that could only raise enthusiasm for the eventful day.

The Royal Procession from Buckingham Palace to St Paul's Cathedral, for a thanksgiving service, passed through gaily-decorated streets. The pavements were crowded with happy, perspiring people all anxious to pay their tribute. In the expensive stands erected along Piccadilly and at other strategic points, grey top-hats were raised as the royal carriage passed, and in the meaner streets, away from the main events, the bunting was festooned from house to house. People danced in the open far into the night; and at each street corner there were flower-decked tables laden with food where children relished a tuck-in. Each street vied with the next to put up a bigger and better show. 'The enthusiasm was most touching' wrote the King in his diary.

Later that week the king and queen drove through the poorer areas of London—Battersea, Kennington, Lambeth, Limehouse, Whitechapel and the Docks—and everywhere the same wholehearted acclamation, the unstinted welcome followed them. The patriotism of working classes surprised some but there was always an explanation. 'They're English, even if they sleep six in a room', commented a member of the judiciary. Each evening the King and Queen appeared on the floodlit balcony of Buckingham Palace. Below them, stretching down the Mall, were their subjects— an animated mass of loyalty packed so close that they could scarcely wave their Union Jacks and streamers. The cheers swelled to a crescendo as the royal couple appeared, to die down when the balcony was empty once more. But they would come out again—just go on calling for them. It was our day as much as theirs.

It was the time when advertising emerged from the conventional era and when eminent artists, not necessarily associated with commerce, contributed to the high standards of many enjoyable advertising campaigns. Advertising was less brash with more humour, and although much of it was dull and commonplace there were brilliant exceptions. Under the direction of Frank Pick, the London Passenger Transport Board produced publicity designs of an incredibly high standard which blazed a trail for others to follow.

There was a romantic approach in Rex Whistler's delicate and charming drawing of a couple picnicking that appeared in the 1930s.

Daisy, Daisy, give me a sandwich do!
Don't be lazy, give me my Guinness, too!
For lunch isn't lunch without it,
So hurry up about it!
It's nice to drink,
And it's nice to think
That a Guinness is good for you.

At that time, too, you could 'Tell the Sergeant-Major that I'll be there in 15 minutes. Explain that I'm just enjoying a CHURCHMAN's No. 1' (10 for 7d; 20 for 1s 2d). A more

64

The Silver Jubilee, 1935. Street scene in Birmingham.

exclusive cigarette was State Express 555 'made by hand one-at-a-time', and to indulge in this luxury it cost all of 2s for twenty-five. The exclusiveness was emphasised by the advertisement showing two or three gentlemen resplendent in white ties and tails looking with surprised pity on an unfortunate individual standing apart from the group who was wearing a *black* tie with tails. 'The man who wore a black tie' the advertisement ran, 'would not be considered "en suite" by his friends. A similar impression is created by the man who smokes and offers cigarettes which fail to tone with his surroundings.' Another advertisement in the series portrayed a man tipping a waiter at a club. For those who had come up the hard way such reminders were doubtless invaluable, and perhaps social gaffes could be mitigated if the

right cigarette for the occasion was offered—not from the packet—but from a suitably expensive case.

Kenneth was comfortably settled in his Buoyant Chair and Miss Mary Brough (who graced the Aldwych farces at that time) posed as a charlady for Robin Starch advertisements. You could also be Sure of Shell, and Mr Therm was blazing a trail even then. In the Underground we were informed that 'Margaret Lockwood affects the heart, Howard's Aspirin does not', and in certain carriages we were not permitted to smoke—'not even Abdullas'. Colman's, the mustard firm, through their agents, S. H. Benson, originated the Mustard Club creating such entertaining characters as the blimpish Baron de Beef and the attractive Miss Di Gester.

The Silver Jubilee, 1935. Their Majesties on the way to St Paul's

"HAROLD, I BELIEVE THEY'RE COMING. PUT YOUR TIE STRAIGHT."

Girls aren't like this any more. The open-air Kodak Girl in the striped dress with the camera—take a look at her camera! 'Nippy' in a Lyon's teashop. She actually took your order and brought it to the table.

The rest? 'The rest is silence—and THREE NUNS the tobacco of curious cut.' In 1931 it cost 1s 3d an ounce but then, possibly, your weekly wage was under £5. And for those in the upper income bracket Fortnum & Mason's Christmas catalogue was a joy to receive. Its presentation and humour made it essential that one should buy *something*, if only to ensure receiving the catalogue next year.

All eyes looked upwards at the aircraft spelling out 'Daily Mail' in smoke against a clear blue sky. On the beach in the summer months we stopped digging sandcastles to watch a low-flying aeroplane move slowly across the sands drawing behind it a banner with the words BILE BEANS. Some of us had 'That Kruschen feeling' which enabled us to leap gates at an advanced age, while Friday night became 'Amami Night' when every working girl washed her hair.

The Ancient Order of Frothblowers existed 'to foster the gentle art and healthy pastime of FROTH BLOWING amongst Gentlemen-of-Leisure and Ex-Soldiers'. On payment of a subscription of 5s, a membership card was supplied and the newly-elected member was permitted to Blow Froth off his own beer 'and occasionally off non-members' beer, provided they are not looking, or of a peaceful disposition'. It was a jolly, let's-all-be-boys-together fraternity

"Tipside Down"

"De Reszke—of course."

"Bother! I've lit my cigarette the wrong end!"

"Calm yourself, child. That's an 'ivory'-tipped De Reszke you've got hold of, and you can go on smoking it even if you have lit it 'tipside down.' You see, these new 'ivory' tips are quite unlike any other tips. They burn just like ordinary cigarette paper, without taste and smell; so lighting up at the wrong end doesn't mean throwing away a first-rate cigarette like these. But next time see that you put the tip end in your mouth, and let your soft lips caress its gleaming ivory-like surface. Then you'll know the uttermost perfection of smoking comfort."

"IVORY"-TIPPED or PLAIN

DE RESZKE

Virginias

20 a shilling

Other De Reszke Cigarettes include *American*, 25 for 1/10; *American de Luxe* (Hand Made), 25 for 2/-; and *Tenor* (Turkish), 25 for 3/2.
You are invited to try any of these cigarettes as our guest at the De Reszke Salon, 86 Piccadilly, London, W.1. (J. Millhoff & Co. Ltd.)

People you don't meet any more. The dashing De Reske type, 'The Major', the discreet 'Jenkyn' (with a 'y'). You don't even meet the brands they promote. No health warnings. 'Make Army Clubs the Health Cigarette', says The Major. 'Smoke Craven "A" for your throat's sake' stated the advertisements in the 1930s

The Officers of the Mustard Club. Back row: *Lord Bacon of Cookham* (address: The Rashers, Cookham); *Master Mustard, Eaton, Bucks; Signor Spaghetti, Parmesan Place, Stoke Doges and Casa Macaroni di Napoli.* Front row: *Miss Di Gester, Secretary of the Club; The Baron de Beef, President of the Club and living at Porterhouse College, Cambridge; Lady Hearty, Tournedos Street, Mayfair, and Gammon Hall, Silverside, Lambshire*

THE OFFICERS OF THE MUSTARD CLUB:

A spread from Fortnum & Mason's 1935 Christmas Catalogue. A delight to the eye and a joy to the taste buds. Smile at the prices, but only the well-to-do could afford them then

C·O·F·F·E·E·S
IN THE BERRY OR GROUND

Roasted Daily on the Premises

AKBAR A blend of the choicest coffee procurable. Its fragrance and delicacy of flavour are as nearly perfect as earthly matters are ever likely to be . . . . *a lb.* 3/8

CABINET The Prince of coffees, certainly one of the happiest blends of rare coffees ever produced . . . . *a lb.* 3/2

KING'S BLEND As supplied to His late Majesty King Edward VII. A very choice coffee . . . . *a lb.* 2/8

BLACK COFFEE "CONNOISSEUR"
Roasted Continental style . . . . . *a lb.* 3/2
AS SERVED IN OUR RESTAURANT

MOCHA Full rich flavour . . . . . *a lb.* 3/2

KENYA Very choice . . . . . . *a lb.* 2/6

Duelists agreed that our stall in St. Martin's Fields contributed largely to the general interests

VISIT
OUR
WINE
CRYPT

24

W·I·N·E·S ETC

PORT
	a doz. bottles
Tawny Port, Medium Colour	52/-
Superior Old Tawny	64/-
"Hunting" Fine Ruby	84/-
"Old Mahogany," Dessert wine	90/-

VINTAGE PORTS
	bottled	*a doz. bottles*
Smith Woodhouse vintage 1920	1922	78/-
Fortnum's Special Selected 1912	1914	125/-
Tuke Holdsworth vintage 1912	1914	155/-
Delaforce 1904	1906	160/-

WHISKY
Fortnum & Mason's Red Seal, fine character, round and full . *a bottle* 12/6

Fortnum & Mason's Fine Old Liqueur (average age 9 years, 25 U.P.) *a bottle* 13/-

SHERRY
	a doz. bottles	46/-
Full Pale		46/-
Manzanilla	,, ,,	54/-
Finest Old Brown	,, ,,	82/-
"Boston Cream"	,, ,,	150/-
Nuez, Old Nutty	,, ,,	58/-

BRANDY
	a bottle
Pale Cognac, 15 years old	17/-
Grande Fine Champagne, vintage 1865	42/-
Grande Fine Champagne, 35 years old	28/-

CHAMPAGNES
	a doz. bottles
Veuve Gallinard, Extra Dry, 1926	112/-
Dieudonné & Cie. Fine Extra Quality	108/-
G. H. Mumm Cordon Rouge 1920	168/-
Louis Roederer, Extra Quality 1926	156/-

GIN
Fortnum & Mason's Finest Old Dry *a bottle* 11/6

VERMOUTH
Fortnum & Mason's French	*a litre* 4/3
Fortnum & Mason's Italian	,, 3/9

PAGE 25

Our famous old cellars have been the haunt of wine lovers since the days of the Regency. They are full of rare and lovely wines

FIRE!

MURDER!

An assistant failing to distract the thoughts of a Connoisseur in our Wine Crypt

70

Membership Card No. 5183

Name _____

Address _____

Do YOU GOLLOP YOUR BEER WITH ZEST?

If so! You are unanimously elected a Member of

Ye Ancient Order of Froth Blowers

Life Membership **5/-** *with all the privileges of the proposed club house, including the use of corkscrews, sawdust, note and other paper, silver cuff-links, etc.*

This ANCIENT GUILD (Circa 1924) exists to foster the noble Art and gentle and healthy Pastime of FROTH BLOWING amongst Gentlemen-of-Leisure and Ex-Soldiers. After payment of Subscription you will be *Permitted* to Blow Froth off your own beer, other members' beer, and occasionally off non-members' beer, provided that they are not looking or are of a peaceful disposition.

Special Privilege :— **IMMUNITY FROM ARREST.**

The Metropolitan Police have been requested not to arrest, annoy, or apprehend any member under or over the influence of Froth, should the said member be wearing the A.O.F.B. cuff links at the time of the debauch.

☞ **"DRINKS ROUND"** ☜
IF NOT WEARING A.O.F.B. LINKS WHEN CHALLENGED.

This book and contents are written and copyrighted by Bert Temple.

A. O. F. B.

'ALE FELLOW, WELL MET!

"STAMPA."

AOFB Membership Card. A 'Blower', a 'Blaster', a 'Monsoon', a 'Grand Typhoon'

initiated by Sir Alfred D. Fripp, KCVO, CB to raise money for his 'Wee Waif' charities. The motto, 'Lubrication in Moderation', the public house setting and the Frothblowers' Anthem:

The more we are together, together, together
The more we are together, the merrier we'll be;
For your friends are my friends
And my friends are your friends
And the more we are together,
The merrier we'll be.

ensured a convivial success for the venture. A member's rating in the Frothblowing fraternity was based on the number of new members he enlisted. A 'Blower' had recruited 1 member,

a 'Blaster' 25, a 'Tornado' 100, a 'Monsoon' 500, while 1,000 recruits made you a 'Grand Typhoon'. There were Frothblower ties (5s 6d), cuff links, handkerchiefs (white 1s, red or blue 6½d), Christmas cards ('order at any W. H. Smith's bookstall or high class stationery dealers') pennants for the car, powder boxes (up to 30s) crackers (4s a box by Tom Smith) etc. In 1927 membership was 232,219 and Sir Alfred Fripp's 'Wee Waif' Children's Charities received up to £15,000 in a single year.

A more individual pastime was the pogo-stick, strictly for the young; adults might try but would hand it back reluctantly to their offspring. In 1922 everyone was frantic over Put and Take. They spun these six-sided tops on

Everyone with a beard was a prospective 'beaver'. Punch *in July, 1922*

every flat surface. Each side of the top was numbered, and they gambled compulsively on which number would turn up. In the thirties Yo-Yo's spun up and down, up and down, but it was the young who mastered them and could do tricks. A flick of the wrist and the Yo-Yo gyrated, twisted and turned. An audience was essential (but not hard to come by) and a blasé expression on the performer's face made it look so easy.

In 1924 a happy pastime was shouting 'beaver' at those sporting beards. Anyone could play at beaver-hunting and did so. It enlivened a dull walk with a companion. An ordinary beard scored one point, but there were numerous varieties, such as a white beard (or polar beaver), that scored more. The winner scored twenty points first; Chelsea Pensioners at that time were in demand.

In 1932 the Rev Harold Davidson, the clean-shaven rector of Stiffkey, was unfrocked because the Norwich Consistory Court failed to agree with his view that the interest he took in girls was fatherly. Later, in Blackpool, he settled down in a barrel on the beach and refused to eat. He continued to exploit his undoubted acting flair, much to the embarrassment of the Establishment, by presenting himself at fairs and exhibitions throughout the country. Even his death in 1937 was spectacular —he was mauled by a lion at Skegness.

The talking point of 1933 was the Loch Ness Monster. The AA Scout who claimed to have seen it sparked off a controversy that continues nearly forty years later. There is less fun now and much more science. Did the creature exist? Rumour abounded. Eminent scientists and important scientific bodies mulled over the evidence and pronounced their verdicts. Books were written, tourists flocked to the area, divers dived, everyone had theories and it was a godsend to the press, not only in England but overseas. And every few years or so, it still is.

The stunts or gimmicks (as they would be called today) diverted thoughts from the problems of the time. Such diversions were welcome, harmless and fun.

Howard Carter (left) and A. C. Mace, discoverers of the Tomb of Tutankhamen in the 1920s

Epstein views his sculpture 'Rima' in memory of W. H. Hudson. Placed in the Bird Sanctuary in Hyde Park it was, said some 'a travesty of nature'. 'Perfect craftsmanship,' said others. It was unveiled in 1925 by Baldwin, then Prime Minister, and periodically covered with tar by vandals

George Lansbury, MP, seen here with the bald head, opened the Lido in Hyde Park in 1930. Mixed bathing in the Serpentine; sunbathing on the banks. Welcomed by the populace but considered a lot of socialist codswallop by some who never made use of the facilities

74

A gigantic blaze puts an end to the Crystal Palace in 1936

'Cockie,' Noel, 'Crazy Words —Crazy Tune'

THEATRE-GOING was still an occasion. Evening performances began (for the most part) at 8.30 giving the theatregoer time to get home from the office, dress and dine. From St John's Wood and other fashionable districts, the cars swept into the West End, the congestion being greatest at Piccadilly Circus where the chauffeur-driven cars queued to drop their passengers at the London Pavilion. If the gaunt face of an unemployed docker peered through the window when the car stopped at a traffic block, this was a momentary unwelcome reminder that must not be allowed to spoil the enjoyment of the evening.

The London Pavilion was the home of the Cochran revue, where many of his most successful and popular productions were to be seen. Whatever C. B. Cochran staged had style and imagination, wit and flair. He attracted talent. A Cochran 'first night' was an occasion. The stalls and dress circle were a-sparkle with white shirt fronts and jewellery, as important for the décor as the stage sets. There was no room for the tawdry and the audience, sensing it, dressed and behaved accordingly. From stage and auditorium there was a delightful rustle of anticipation of the entrancing evening ahead. Talent came in the form of writers like Noël Coward and Cole Porter. Designers (Gladys Calthrop), choreographers (Tilly

Losch) and a multitude of actors and actresses made their names with Cochran whose genius lay in recognising talent and providing the best framework and atmosphere for its flowering.

Noël Coward's material above all portrayed the age. As he emphasises the theatre is primarily a place for entertainment and it was entertainment in the truest sense of the word that emerged during that period. As Jessie Matthews and Sonnie Hale sang in *This Year of Grace*:

> *A room with a view—and you,*
> *And no-one to worry us . . .*

or again Gertrude Lawrence singing in *Private Lives*:

> *Some day I'll find you*
> *Moonlight behind you . . .*

created a romantic atmosphere that people craved for in the late 1920s after the deprivations of the war. Then, in the mid-1930s as the possibility of a new war increased, the more frantic:

> *Play, orchestra, play*
> *Play something light and sweet and gay*
> *For we must have music,*
> *We must have music*
> *To drive our fears away*

from *To-night at 8.30*, the group of plays under that umbrella title which was presented by John C. Wilson (not Cochran). The song was sung by Gertrude Lawrence.

It was all right to poke fun at the empire builders in 'Mad dogs and Englishmen' and their inclination to go out in the mid-day sun, or to portray the landed gentry in 'The Stately Homes of England', as long as it was done light-heartedly. These pin-pricks at the social standards and conventions of the day were all *so* amusing and *so* true, but making fun of a situation didn't mean anything had to *change*, did it? The audience roared their approval and

Noël Coward and Gertrude Lawrence with (left) Frederic March and (right) Douglas Fairbanks Jr

the songs were sung and danced to at all the smart parties and night clubs, for not only were the words appropriate and frequently very funny, but the tunes had a compulsive lilt.

The revue was spectacular, topical and witty. There was singing, dancing and delightful costumes. The chorus was attractive and from its ranks emerged future stars. C. B. Cochran always looked at a girl's ankles before he looked at her face, but 'Mr Cochran's Young Ladies' could not only dance, they could also sing and look glamorous. The revue was a frothy concoction. Cochran's presentations were spectacular but intimate; André Charlot and Albert de Courville concentrated more on the *revue de grand spectacle*.

Buzz-buzz at the Vaudeville in December

1918 was one of the first popular revues after the war. It ran for over 600 performances and featured Gertrude Lawrence and Nelson ('Call me Bunch') Keys. In 1923 Lupino Lane and Billy Merson appeared in *Brighter London* which included the famous sketch of them cleaning the face of Big Ben. There were numerous editions and changes of material in *Charlot's Revue* which first opened at the Prince of Wales and among those that appeared in the various versions were Henry Kendall, Phyllis Monkman, Maisie Gay, Beatrice Lillie, Jack Buchanan and Dorothy Dickson. Jack Hulbert and Cicely Courtneidge were in *Clowns in Clover* at the Adelphi, which included the latter's famous sketch in which she attempted to buy from Harridge's Linen Department

(left) Ruth Draper. Her only stage prop was a chair, yet one could 'see' a host of characters she created; (right) Carl Brisson, star of Wonderbar *(1930) and every girl's pin-up*

during a Great White Sale, 'two dozen double damask dinner napkins' and got hopelessly and uproariously tongue-tied in the process.

A show called *The Co-optimists* opened in the heatwave of June 1921 at the Royalty Theatre. It cost £950 to put on and was a sophisticated version of a pier seaside concert party. Each Co-optimist introduced himself (or herself) in an opening number.

> *My name is one you can't forget,*
> *Your memory cannot fail*
> *You've only got to think of pills*
> *An ointment, gin and gaol*

sang Stanley Holloway. Other members of the company included Davy Burnaby (a slightly less robust version of Fred Emney), and Phyllis Monkman, while at the piano Melville Gideon revealed:

> *They cannot do without me,*
> *As you must plainly see*
> *Where'er they go, they'll always be*
> *Accompanied by me.*

It ran for over 500 performances and was revived in 1927. The famous Dolly Sisters appeared in Cochran's *League of Notions* at the

New Oxford in 1921. *London Calling* was an André Charlot revue at the Duke of York's, with lyrics and music by Noël Coward (who also appeared in it with Maisie Gay and Gertrude Lawrence). A sketch entitled 'The Swiss Family Whittlebot' burlesqued the Sitwells much to their displeasure. Nellie Wallace of music hall fame appeared with Arthur Riscoe in *Sky High* at the Palladium in 1925, and Gracie Fields was to be seen in *The Show's the Thing* at the Victoria Palace in 1929. *Pot Luck* at the Vaudeville in 1921 will be remembered for Gwen Farrar and Norah Blaney, the 'cellist and pianist respectively, whose musical talent was equalled by their wit. The spectacular *Blackbirds* —the coloured revue from America—featured Florence Mills and the famous song 'Bye Bye Blackbird'.

The 'intimate' revue, staged in a small theatre, became popular in 1938 and 1939. What it lacked in spectacle, it made up for in wit, topicality and sophistication. It appealed to what would now be termed the 'in' crowd. The Little Theatre in John Street, Adelphi holding a mere 350 people was the obvious setting for the 'intimate' revue. *The Little Revue, Nine Sharp* (indicating the hour the performance began, giving the audience time to be well dressed and dined and to enter the theatre in a cloud of cigar smoke and with a feeling of well-being) were inspired by Herbert Farjeon. These revues featured George Benson, Cyril Ritchard and Hermione Baddeley. At the Ambassador's *The Gate Revue* (and later, *Swinging the Gate*) was presided over by Hermione Gingold. The seemingly acid exchanges between the two Hermiones—Baddeley and Gingold—date from these intimate revue days.

There were plays with a message. Sherriff's *Journey's End* in 1929 remains one of the few

(*left*) *Jack Buchanan, star of many musicals. He sang and danced with—*
(*right*) *Elsie Randolph. Here they are in* Mr Whittington (*1934*)

The Gate Revue *at the Ambassadors in 1939, originally produced at the Gate Theatre. The 'intimate' revue became popular shortly before World War II. The humour was satirical, sophisticated, sharp and subtle.* Left to right: *Gabrielle Brun, Michael Wilding, Hermione Gingold, Walter Crisham, Doris Gilmore, Jack McNaughton*

plays dealing with the Great War in a manner that was theatrically successful. John van Druten's *Young Woodley* (with Frank Lawton and Frances Doble), a study of adolescence in a school setting, created a sensation when it was produced in 1928. Originally banned by the censor, it was first put on by the Stage Society as a protest against the decision. Noël Coward's *The Vortex* originally staged at the Everyman in Hampstead in 1924 established Coward as a playwright but the confrontation of son and drug-taking mother on the stage was more than could be accepted by some at that time. 'Un peu schoking' as James Agate wrote in his *Sunday Times* review.

The Aldwych made theatre history by its series of successful farces (mostly by Ben Travers) with Ralph Lynn and Tom Walls. *A Cuckoo in the Nest, Tons of Money, Thark* were some of the more popular ones. Lynn was the silly ass with monocle; Walls the sporty type. As often as not there was J. Robertson Hare exclaiming 'Oh misery me' and being pushed into cupboards and embarrassing situations. It was a brilliant team of talent (Winifred Shotter often playing the damsel in distress) which had the Aldwych rocking to its foundations with laughter.

Musical comedy was the popular light entertainment. Thin in plot with a slender romantic story, it threaded its way through a welter of misunderstanding at the end of the second act, to the final curtain fall on a happy-ever-after ending. At the slightest opportunity such action as there was halted, and a song was sung. It was less sophisticated than the revue. The boy-meets-girl in tuneful circumstances was the formula much loved by the middle classes.

Edith Day in *Irene* at the Empire immortalised the 'Alice Blue Gown' song in 1920. *Lilac Time* opened at the Lyric two years later. *Rose Marie*, at Drury Lane in 1926 with Edith Day as the star and Anna Neagle in the chorus, ran for over 800 performances. A year before *No, No, Nanette* opened at the Palace with George Grossmith, Joe Coyne and Binnie Hale, and there wasn't an errand boy who didn't whistle 'Tea for Two', not a bathroom that failed to resound to:

I want to be happy,
But I can't be happy
Till I make you happy, too.

It was Binnie Hale who explained to Bobby Howes in *Mr Cinders* that she was 'a one-man girl who's looking for a one-girl man'. Harry Welchman and Edith Day sang their way through *The Desert Song* at Drury Lane in 1927; and close by at the now demolished Winter Garden Theatre, Derek Oldham and Winnie Melville joined voices in *The Vagabond King*. The Theatre Royal, Drury Lane was splendid for the spectacular musical. The revolving stage, the opportunities for massive sets and scenes enabled the ambitious *Show Boat* to be staged there in 1928. Paul Robeson's 'Ole Man River' became a classic. The Coliseum,

The cast that filled the Aldwych for years in a series of farces, mostly by Ben Travers.
Left to right: Mary Brough being throttled by Ralph Lynn, Winifred Shotter,
J. Robertson Hare, Tom Walls, Ethel Coleridge and Gordon James. Here they are
in Thark *(1927)*

also suitably equipped for the spectacular, was the home from 1931 for many years, of *The White Horse Inn.*

Noël Coward's *Bitter Sweet* with Peggy Wood and Ivy St Helier ran for nearly 700 performances at His Majesty's Theatre, containing the famous song.

> *I'll see you again,*
> *Whenever Spring breaks through again*

Ivor Novello was the star of the romantic musical-comedy world. He wrote the words and the music, and often played the principal part. With his brand of sentimental, escapist romance, he and Mary Ellis packed Drury Lane in 1935 with *Glamorous Night*, and a year later with Dorothy Dickson and *Careless Rapture* at the same theatre. *The Dancing Years* opened the year war broke out. In another vein *Me and My Girl* with Lupino Lane and Teddie St Denis filled the Victoria Palace from 1937 for 1,646 performances, with its cockney whelk-stall appeal and the Lambeth Walk to immortalise it.

The music hall was not killed yet. The Palladium, the Holborn Empire, the Metropolitan, Edgware Road and for a time the Coliseum billed Nellie Wallace, Billy (Almost a Gentleman) Bennett, George Robey and a host of lesser acts individually enjoyable and polished. It was Billy Bennett who used to come to the front of the stage and announce with mock solemnity: 'Recitation entitled "Mother open the window, I want to throw out my chest",' and Nellie Wallace who sang, 'My Mother said Always Look Under the Bed' but lamented she'd never 'found a man there yet'.

Such entertainment remained the staple diet of the provincial towns and cities until the 'talkies' reduced the number of music halls from hundreds to scores. In order to meet the competition, the music hall discarded its

No, No, Nanette (1925) *with* (left to right) *Binnie Hale, George Grossmith, Joseph Coyne* (on sofa), *Seymour Beard, Irene Brown, Marie Hemingway*

(*left*) *Binnie Hale in* Mr Cinders *at the Adelphi in 1929;* (*right*) *Ivor Novello, author and composer of many romantic musicals*—Glamorous Night (*1935*), Careless Rapture (*1936*), The Dancing Years (*1939*)

traditional role and attempted novelties such as non-stop variety which watered down the quality. Only the Windmill succeeded in this respect, and became the launching pad for many famous radio and television comedians. Possibly the only check in the steady decline of the music hall was *Crazy Week* which began in 1932 at the Palladium and eventually developed into *The Crazy Gang*. Jimmy Nervo and Teddy Knox, Charles Naughton and Jimmy Gold, 'Monsewer' Eddie Gray and Bud Flanagan and Chesney Allen were all members of the hilarious gang at one time or another.

But even the *Crazy Gang* was a diversion. Nothing could revive the music hall. It was no longer needed. A joke or act that could last for years in the music hall was told once-and-for-

all on the radio. The reluctance to loosen the grip on a microphone and the inability to make oneself heard without it, so restricted movement that the old music-hall artistes retired to rest homes in disgust with the sure knowledge that nobody would ever see their like again.

Then the songs. The scores of the musical shows were murdered on an upright piano in the front room, the pianist picking out with one finger the tune of what was charmingly called the 'refrain'. Round the piano family and guests assembled for a sing-song (especially at Christmas) and the room filled with the sound of voices—'Good Bye-ee, Don't cry-ee' or possibly 'K-k-k-Katy, Beautiful Katy' or 'Last Night on the Back Porch'—there was a multitude too numerous to mention.

We bought records to put on our portable gramophone, turning the handle to wind it up after each record. The tone wasn't all that good but 'Ramona', 'You're the Cream in my Coffee' and 'Tip-toe through the Tulips' came across to our satisfaction. Later the dance bands on the wireless played the hit numbers from the latest shows. Later still, the spectacular 'talkie' musicals were the source of an additional flow of popular songs such as 'Broadway Melody' and '42nd Street'.

Each summer, when the London 'season' was in full swing and there were dances night after night, three or four tunes became the rage. Throughout the autumn and winter their popularity continued, but by next summer other tunes were the craze. But the deposed ones did not disappear entirely. They were still 'requested' by last year's couples. They are still remembered and a song or tune can bring back a flood of memories—some hilarious, some sad, some poignant.

Wilson, Keppel and Betty in the music-hall sketch Cleopatra's Nightmare. *An hilarious sand dance in a popular act that toured the world over. They came to the Palladium in 1932*

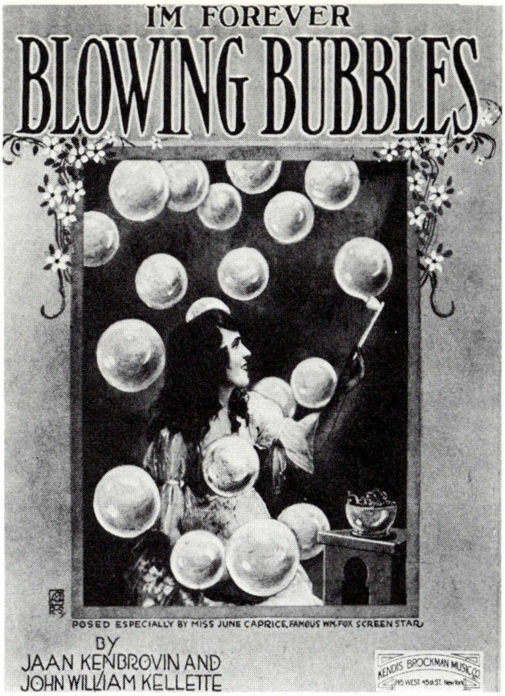

1919

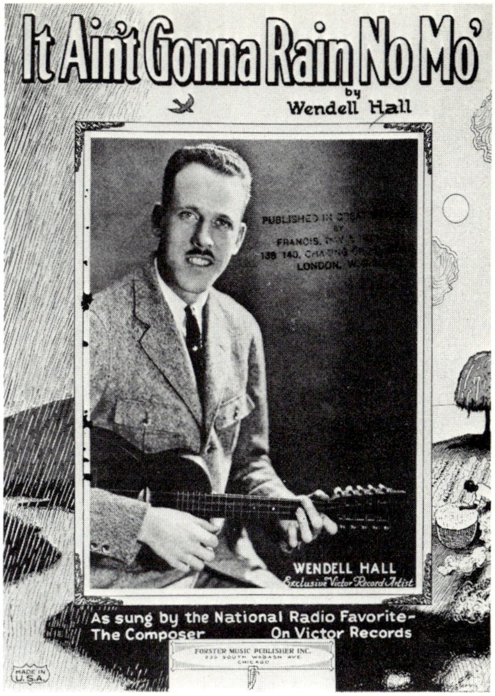

1924

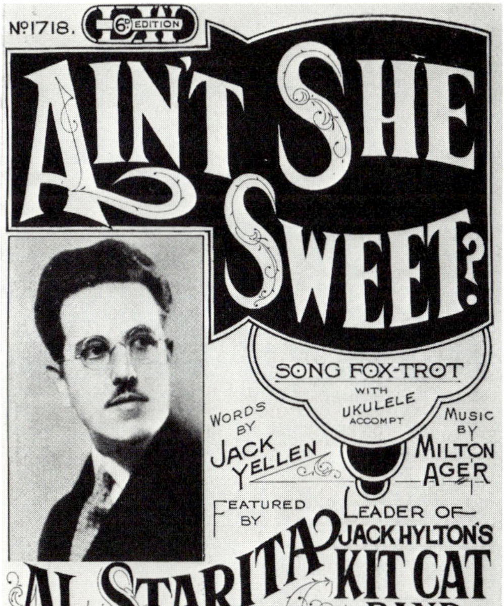

1927

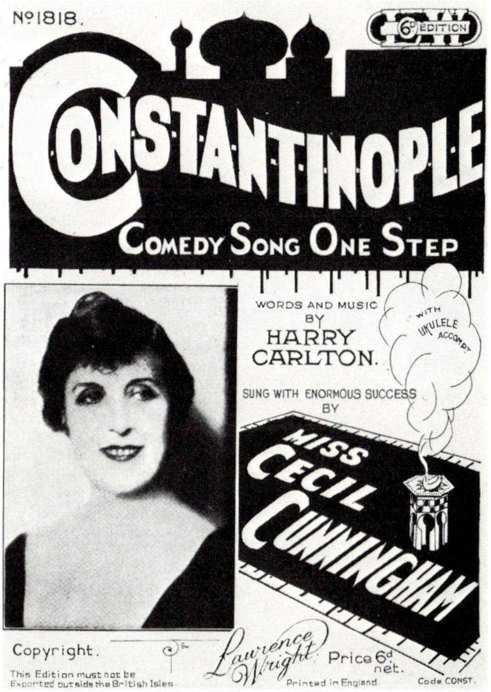

1928

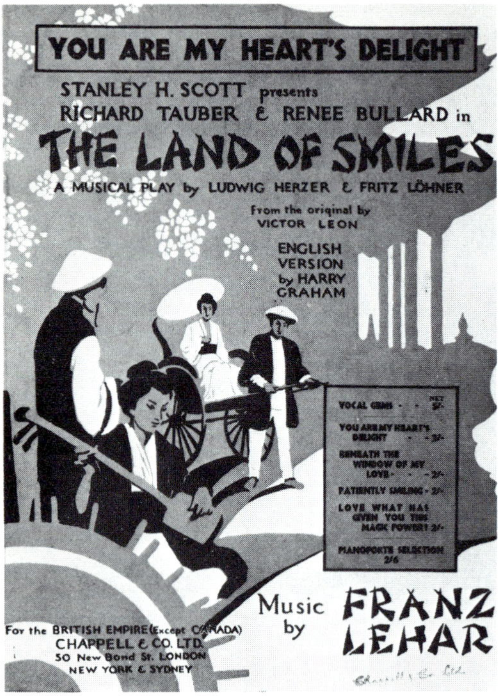

1931

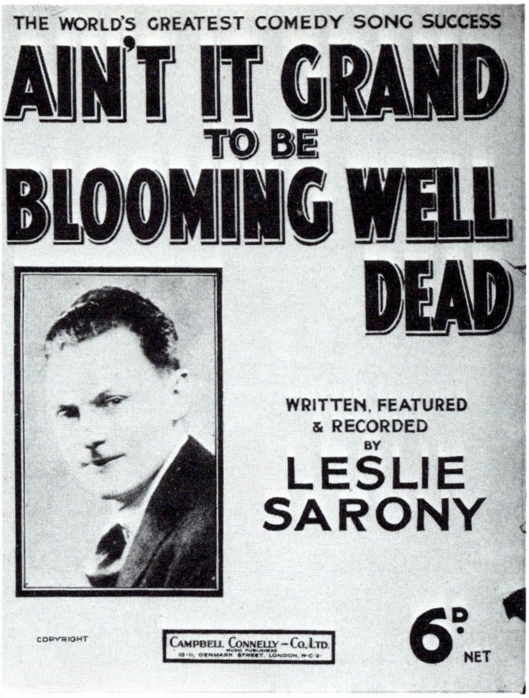

1932

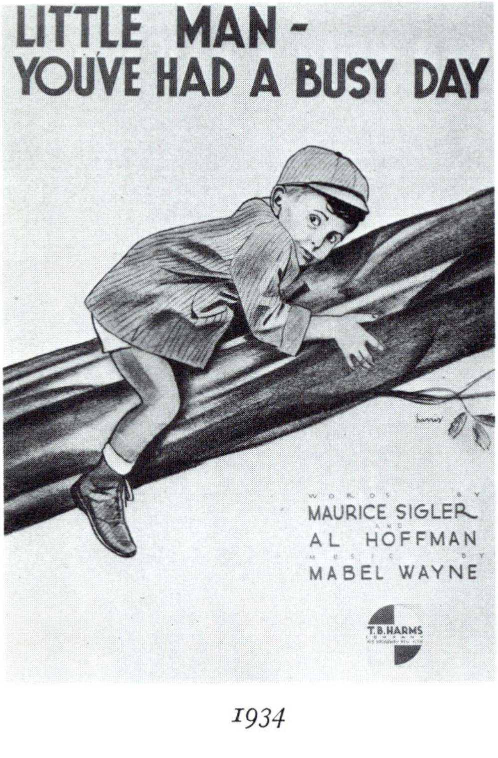

1934

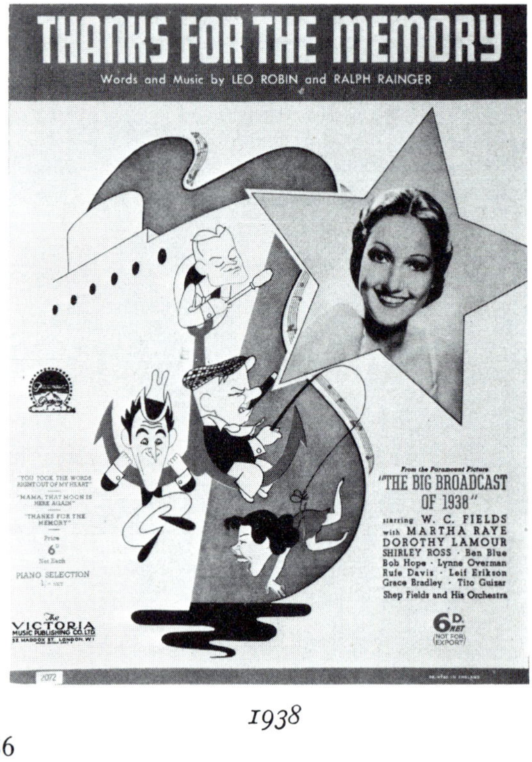

1938

Flying High and the Tin Lizzie

A FINE Sunday morning (not Saturday morning because we were working then) and the feeling that it would be nice to motor down to the coast, no thoughts of parking restrictions or traffic problems, just pack up lunch and away. Away in what? Henry Ford's Tin Lizzie, the wheels with detachable rims and a spare rim and tyre on the running board? Or the bull-nose Morris-Cowley, a gauge fixed to the bonnet which showed when things were likely to boil over? Possibly it was the Austin Seven (costing £165) launched in 1922, in which driver and passengers were exposed to the vagaries of the British climate which a hood did little to alleviate. Or would you have passed everything on the road in your 20hp Rolls Royce? It was the era of the light car—the 10–12hp class—and of names such as Calcott, Calthorpe, Clyno, Cluley, Swift and Stellite which have now disappeared from the scene.

In the twenties the roads were free from traffic. It was possible and pleasant to stop by the road-side and picnic, but by the end of the twenties the patterns of future chaos were in evidence. Traffic at seaside resorts at the height of the holiday season was becoming a problem,

The Driver. "WHAT DO YOU THINK OF THOSE LITTLE THINGS?"
The Passenger. "MAKE TOPPING ASH-TRAYS."

It was the era of the light car. Punch *in 1927*

THE INVENTIVE SIDE OF MOTORDOM:
INTERESTING NOVELTIES IN DESIGN.

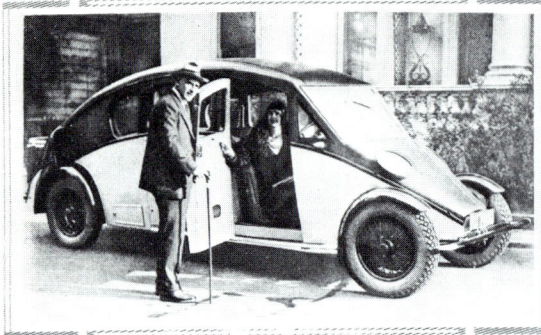

A FAMOUS AIRSHIP-BUILDER AS MOTOR-CAR DESIGNER: SIR DENNISTOUN BURNEY AND LADY BURNEY WITH HIS UNIQUE CAR OF STREAMLINED FORM, BUILT TO HIS OWN SPECIFICATIONS.

ANOTHER DISTINCTIVE FEATURE OF THE NEW TYPE OF CAR DESIGNED BY SIR DENNISTOUN BURNEY: THE ENGINE PLACED AT THE BACK, INSTEAD OF IN FRONT.

AN INNOVATION TO PREVENT DRAUGHTS WHILE PROVIDING VENTILATION: THE REAR WINDOWS OF THE "VORTIC" HILLMAN SALOON OPENING TOWARDS THE BACK.

AN INGENIOUSLY CONSTRUCTED SIDE LOCKER FOR CARRYING TOOLS INSIDE A RECEPTACLE FOR A SPARE WHEEL: A NEW FITTING IN THE 40-50-H.P. ROLLS-ROYCE WITH BARKER BODY.

ANOTHER NOVELTY IN THE 40-50-H.P. ROLLS-ROYCE WITH BARKER BODY: A FOLDING STEP THAT OPENS AND CLOSES WITH THE DOOR.

A DEVICE THAT WILL APPEAL TO GOLFERS: A HUMBER COUPÉ WITH A SPECIAL COMPARTMENT FOR GOLF-CLUBS IN THE SIDE.

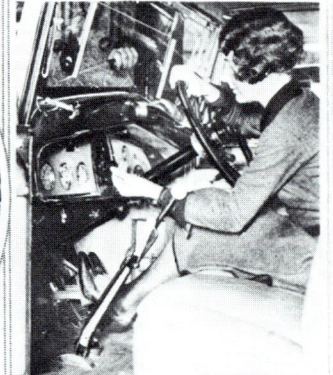

FOR THE WOMAN MOTORIST WHO LIKES MUSIC ALL THE WAY: A WIRELESS SET FITTED TO THE INSTRUMENT-BOARD OF AN ISOTTA-FRASCHINI.

Innovations in 1930 that made motoring more comfortable

and the traffic block in the major towns and cities had now to be reckoned with. Rules and regulations were necessary and they came with increasing frequency: white lines, traffic signals (in St James's Street, London, in 1926), gyratory traffic schemes and one-way streets (both at Hyde Park Corner in 1926) and Belisha Beacons, initiated by Leslie Hore-Belisha in 1934 when he was Minister of Transport. King George V opened the Great West Road in May 1935, and in the same year the new Southend road was in use. The North Circular and the Kingston By Pass relieved the pressure on the main trunk roads out of London. Further afield the Glasgow–Inverness road was improved, and a new road through the Pass of Glencoe constructed. The Edinburgh–Glasgow road was created partly out of existing roads, and the east Lancashire towns were served by a new road from Liverpool in 1928. The Liverpool–Birkenhead road tunnel under the Mersey was finished, and bridges over the Tyne at Newcastle and the Tweed at Berwick were opened in 1928.

The increasing popularity of the motor car resulted in a rash of new garages and filling stations. No longer was it necessary to carry a two-gallon petrol can in the car. Now the petrol pump, with its illuminated glass globe beckoned the motorist to fill up at less than 2s a gallon. In the twenties the pumps were worked manually, but by the thirties electric pumps were in use.

Eventually the car became more weatherproof, largely due to the introduction of mass-production methods, making it simpler to turn out saloon models. For those who felt the need of fresh air, there was the 'sunshine' roof which could be pulled back to let in whatever sun and fresh air were available. Unfortunately it also let in the rain.

The racing enthusiasts went to Brooklands—the only circuit available until Donnington Park opened in the thirties. In 1924 at Pendine, Malcolm Campbell in his Sunbeam achieved the land speed record of 146·16mph, which was beaten in 1927 at Daytona by Henry Segrave at 200mph in his 1,000hp Sunbeam. In 1935 at Bonneville Salt Pans, Malcolm Campbell recorded 301·13mph, but the six-wheeled *Thunderbolt* powered by two supercharged Rolls-Royce engines and driven by George Eyston raised the record to 357mph in Utah in 1938.

There was a craze among the Bright Young Things for organising treasure hunts by car. The driver of each car—and there might be a dozen or so, filled with passengers—was handed a clue, possibly in verse, which, when solved,

Eventually the car became more weatherproof—for those inside. Fougasse comments in Punch *in 1926*

A Ladies' Rally

indicated where the next clue was to be found. The cars raced off—speed was essential—to pick up the new clue, possibly ten or more miles away, hidden in a tree trunk, or concealed near a milestone or ancient monument. The winner, rushing to the final hiding place, collected his 'treasure' in the shape of a bottle or bottles, which would be shared with his passengers. The races between competitors—even on the quiet roads—could be hair-raising, but it was a way of spending what might have otherwise been a dreary Sunday.

The internal combustion engine was taking over from the horse. In 1922 there were some 22,000 horse-drawn vehicles and 975,000 motor vehicles. In 1930 the horse-drawn vehicles numbered about 52,000, motor vehicles over 2 million. The increased traffic on the roads ousted the tram. The clanging bell and the familiar rumble were noises that were to disappear. The tramlines were skid hazards in wet weather and it was becoming difficult to squeeze large motor vehicles between the pavements and the trams.

The danger to passengers who had to enter and leave a tram from the roadway was a hazard in a period of rising accidents, and the impatient motorist who had to wait in the traffic block while the tram collected and disgorged its passengers added to the difficulties. The trackless trolley bus, powered from the overhead tram wires, had the advantage of being able to pull into the kerb. But frequently the arm came off the wires and had to be manually replaced, so that the vehicle became a solid obstacle in a sea of whirling motor traffic.

The bus services were catering for the increased mobility of the nation. Eastern Counties, formed in 1919, was carrying in 1926 nearly 5 million passengers in seventy-eight buses. The United Automobile Services of York covered 2,000 route-miles in 1929, while the Thames Valley Traction Company in 1927 carried 9 million passengers with its 141 vehicles. In London, directly after the war, the double decker open bus was in use. Riding outside was bracing, exposed as one was to the rain, sleet and fog. A tarpaulin cover, fixed to each row of seats, and placed over the knees kept the lower garments dry until one stood up to get off the bus. Then the rain that had collected in the tarpaulin cascaded down over one's clothes. Although the London General Omnibus Company covered most of the routes there was the occasional 'pirate' bus service which weaved its way in and out of the traffic to pick up passengers before the 'General' came along. There were no 'request' stops. The bus could be hailed anywhere along the route. The formation of the London Passenger Transport Board in 1933 eliminated the 'pirates' and tightened up route discipline.

London's Underground (eventually incorporated into the London Passenger Transport Board) extended the Hampstead line to Edgware in 1924, and the Piccadilly line continued to Uxbridge and Harrow in 1932, and from Finsbury Park to Cockfosters the following year. The Metropolitan Railway electrified the line from Harrow to Rickmansworth and extended it to Watford in 1925. 'Metroland', the rural area covered by the Metropolitan Railway, was a haven for the middle classes. 'To obtain the quickest access to open country is the aim of the majority of those who have business and social interests in the Metropolis', stated an estate agent's brochure of the 1920s. Houses could be bought for £1,000 or less. There was a shopping centre nearby with W. H. Smith's, the International Stores, the Fifty-Shilling Tailors possibly, and a bank. There was no need to wander far from 'The Elms' or 'Shangri-La'. The neatly tended gardens were to be admired, the clean white curtains at the windows discouraged further inquiries.

The railways, after the war effort, needed a period of recovery. Trains such as the *Cheltenham Flyer*, the *Silver Jubilee* (London–Newcastle), the *Coronation* (London–Edinburgh) and the *Coronation Scot* (London–Glasgow), achieved speeds and time-schedules which did much to restore popularity. These and an intelligent attempt to provide trains in the right place at the right time with restaurant

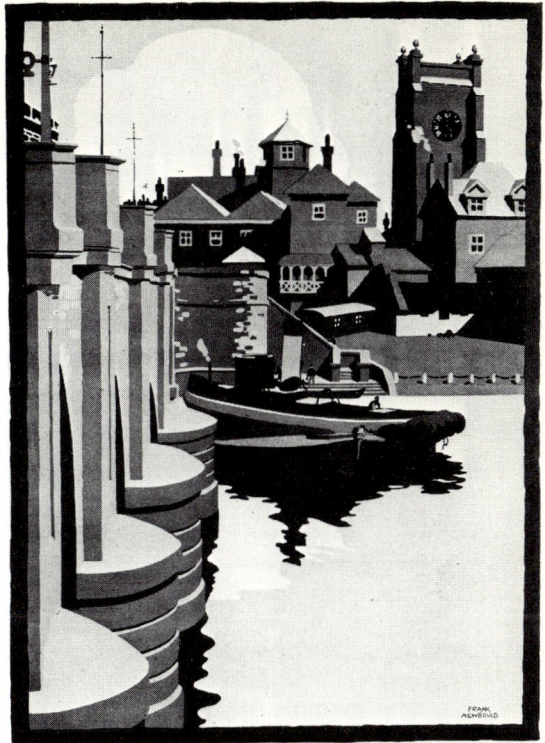

Kingston by tram

1925

facilities, helped them to compete with other forms of transport, although the virtual monopoly of the railways was at an end.

In 1921 some 120 lines, such as the London, Brighton & South Coast Railway, were incorporated into four regional groups—the London, Midland & Scottish, the London & North Eastern, the Great Western and the Southern. While such a move might make for greater efficiency, it was felt that the passenger would lose out by having to deal with a 'region' rather than an individual 'line'. Competition was being stifled. In spite of co-ordination the railways lost money and in the thirties some 900 miles of line were closed, increasing the reliance of the population on the motor car and the bus.

What was the matter with one's own two feet? Nothing, and the thirties were the era of the hiking boom. Hikers' Leagues and Clubs were founded, many encouraged and sponsored by the national and provincial press. 'Metroland', taking in Wembley, Harrow and Rickmansworth, was still a good area for walks and could be reached quickly. The railways organised special excursions. A 'Mystery Express' took hikers, unaware of their destination, out into the country, let them hike for a few hours and then rejoin the train for home. A moonlight walk over the Sussex Downs to witness the sunrise from Chanctonbury Ring captured the imagination of the more romantic. In 1930 the Youth Hostels Association was founded. Others liked to be independent of accommodation and carried, in addition to a change of clothing, cooking materials, a primus stove and oilskin tents. The dress was similar for both sexes—shorts, open-neck shirts and on the head a beret at an angle that was strangely unbecoming. It was not an outfit that always flattered the wearer, but collectively most people got by.

It was a means of getting away from the increasingly stifling cities. As the years went by, it was necessary to go further and further afield. 'Metroland', for example, had lost most of its fields and pathways by World War II. In their place were houses, and with better transport the new owners of these homes crowded into the trains to work in London. The mortgage had to be paid.

The air was relatively unexplored. There were vast distances to be covered by aircraft,

1932—the hiking season begins. Wet Waterloo Station is a starting point for, one hopes, sunnier spots. Note the plus fours on the extreme left

Pioneers of the air: (*above left*) *Earhart;* (*above right*) *Alcock and Brown;* (*below left*) *Lindbergh;* (*below right*) *Mollison*

Travel by AIR

The quickest, safest, and most comfortable way to travel between London and the Continent is by

IMPERIAL
AIRWAYS

THE ONLY BRITISH AIR LINE TO AND FROM THE CONTINENT.

THE machines used by Imperial Airways are all of the very latest British design. They are manned by highly skilled and experienced British Pilots—the best in the world. Each machine is fitted with wireless and luxuriously equipped to ensure the complete comfort of passengers. Imperial Airways is the only air line in the world which has its machines inspected before each journey by men holding Government Certificates. In fact everything that is humanly possible, is done to ensure safety, speed and comfort.

All fares on Imperial Airways include motor car conveyance between the Company's starting points and the Aerodromes. Motor cars await incoming passengers at all Aerodromes. London passengers are picked up at Hotel Victoria, Northumberland Avenue for Croydon Aerodrome and Paris passengers at Hotel Crillon for Bourget Aerodrome. Passengers are allowed 30 lbs. personal luggage. Excess luggage is carried or sent in advance at a moderate charge.

TO send letters by air, it is only necessary to go to the nearest Post Office and hand in the letters at the counter, all such correspondence being plainly marked " By Air Mail." The surcharge is very small, and information can be obtained from any Post Office as to the times for mailing. With regard to parcels, you can either put these through the parcel mail at the Post Office marked " By Air Mail " ; or, if too large for parcels post, they can be collected by freight agents and dispatched in the usual manner. Arrangements can also be made to carry legal and other documents by air for signature, and then for their return to the sender. For full particulars of Freight rates, or in fact *anything* you want to know about Air Travel or Transport—Ring up CROYDON 2046.

The Central Booking Office is at Croydon Aerodrome, but seats may be booked at all the usual Travel Agencies in England and Abroad.

IMPERIAL AIRWAYS LTD., The Air Port of London, CROYDON.

Ring up CROYDON 2046.

Telegrams : "FLYING, CROYDON."

Travel by IMPERIAL AIRWAYS from LONDON
to PARIS, BASLE, ZURICH, OSTEND, BRUSSELS, COLOGNE, AMSTERDAM, HANOVER or BERLIN and from SOUTHAMPTON to GUERNSEY
or vice versa.

C.F.H.

An Imperial Airways advertisement of 1924 with instructions as to how letters should be sent by air

Flying to Paris. The passenger door was low enough not to need steps

and pioneers such as Alcock and Brown, Alan Cobham, Jim Mollison, Charles Lindbergh and others flew their ill-equipped and flimsy craft across thousands of miles to distant continents. Women, too, such as Amy Johnson, Amelia Earhart, Jean Batten flew solo over stretches of sea and land severed from all communication with the ground for long periods of time. These exploits were featured in, and often sponsored by, the press, and readers followed the progress and adventures of these pioneer flyers. Engine trouble or other mishaps, such as running out of petrol, could mean disaster. Somehow they kept airborne and achieved their destinations, where, weary almost beyond endurance, they were acclaimed by crowds that had waited hours to see them.

In February 1919 a Department of Civil Aviation within the British Air Ministry was established. By November, it was possible to send letters air mail to Paris. In April 1924 Imperial Airways began a daily London to Paris passenger service; eleven years later there was a daily service between London, Brussels, Cologne, Prague, Vienna and Budapest. In 1937 the Imperial Airways flying boat *Centaurus* flew from Britain to New Zealand. Weather, which today could be ignored, grounded aircraft. There were delays and discomforts, but informality and a feeling of adventure prevailed. Unexpected hazards had to be overcome; to have been up in an aeroplane was something to boast about.

In July 1919 the first airship—the R34—crossed the Atlantic from Scotland to New York and back to Norfolk, but this achievement was followed by disasters. The R38 broke up during trials over Hull in 1921 and crashed;

forty-three lives were lost. In 1930 the R101 on a flight to Egypt and India hit a hill near Beauvais in France. On crashing it burst into flames, and forty-seven of the fifty-two passengers and crew were killed including Lord Thompson, Secretary of State for Air, and Sir Sefton Brancker, Director of Civil Aviation. This disaster ended airship development in Britain for many years.

But people were on the move. The motor car was crowding the roads and there were developments up in the skies that would enable the insular Englishman to travel to lands that had hitherto been names on a map.

Cricket, Carnera and the First Wembley Cup Final

LEISURE WAS to be enjoyed by watching other people work hard at sport. The cricket match on the village green, the Saturday afternoon rugby football turn-out, golf and bowls for those of more advanced years were pleasurable occupations, but the less energetic preferred to join huge crowds and watch the skilful experts. It was the beginning of the cult of the hero-sportsman.

On the cricket field Jack Hobbs, Frank Woolley and Wilfred Rhodes created records that are still talked about with bated breath. Holmes and Sutcliffe, with their record partnership of 555 runs for Yorkshire against Essex at Leyton in 1932 were besieged by enthusiasts for autographs. The county championship was eagerly fought, Yorkshire winning it twelve times between 1919 and 1939, and Lancashire five. In 1926 England won the Ashes from Australia for the first time since 1920 by winning the exciting final Test at the Oval; all the

other matches had been draws. The 'bodyline' crisis—and crisis it seemed—became the highlight of the 1933 Test Matches in Australia under the captaincy of D. R. Jardine. Harold Larwood of Nottingham was accused of 'bodyline' bowling—a ball that drops short and rises to the batsman's head. Don Bradman, captain of the Australians, had seen Woodfall and Oldfield struck by balls from Larwood and there was an angry reaction from the crowd. Hitler might be in control of Germany, but 'bodyline' bowling was something that concerned the Empire. The word 'unsportsmanlike' had been bandied about. There was talk of curtailing the tour. Cables between the cricketing bodies in England and Australia were given the attention of important diplomatic exchanges concerning a war, but tempers eased and the press found new crises to blow up.

On the cricket playing fields, it was the day of the amateur and professional cricketer. The

96

Jack Hobbs. He beat W. G. Grace's record of 126 centuries

Like so many ants. The scene at the first Cup Final at Wembley Stadium when the crowds broke the barriers and swarmed over the pitch

(*above*) *Bolton Wanderers, Cup Winners 1928–9*. Back row: *Kean, Howarth, Parry (Reserve), Pym, Seddon, Finney*. Front row: *Butler, McClelland, Blackmore, Gibson, Murphy, Nuttall*. (*below*) *Joe Davis* (right) *with Lindrum striking for break at the New Holborn Billiard Hall, 1930*

'Gentlemen', as the amateurs were known, had their initials printed before their surnames on the score cards; the professionals or 'Players' after. Thus when F. T. Mann and Hearne, J. W. T. returned to the pavilion at Lords after playing on the field together, the former used the front entrance, the latter the entrance at the side. Likewise P. G. H. Fender and Hobbs, J. B. approached the Oval pavilion at different angles. A Player was not suitable 'captain of the side' material unless there was no possible amateur. The 'Gentlemen v Players' matches played each season helped to perpetuate such social differences.

Association Football was professional and made no pretensions otherwise. In 1922 S. Puddefoot (West Ham) was transferred to Falkirk for £5,000. In 1928 David Jack (Bolton) went to Arsenal for nearly £11,000 and ten years later Jones (Wolves) was welcomed by Arsenal for £14,000. Arsenal were the Football League First Division Champions more times than any other team between the wars; although Bolton Wanderers won the Cup Final more often. The first radio commentary on a Cup Final was in 1929 when Bolton Wanderers beat Portsmouth 2-0. In 1930 the Football Association forbade floodlit football, and six years later issued a report condemning Pools Football betting.

The first Cup Final at Wembley Stadium between Bolton Wanderers and West Ham United nearly ended in disaster. The queues which formed at the turnstiles—there must have been 150,000 people—were orderly at first until it was realised that not all would get in to see the game. Many broke into the Stadium, the pitch was filled with milling people and there was the greatest difficulty in getting the ground cleared so that the game could proceed. Fortunately there were no casualties, but as a result admission to future Cup Final matches was by ticket.

Suzanne Lenglen—dynamic, temperamental—won the Women's Singles at Wimbledon from 1919-23 and in 1925

Billiards was popular, and Joe Davis was the Professional United Kingdom Billiards Champion from 1934-9; the runner-up was always Tom Newman. Tom Newman had been the World Professional Champion six times between 1919 and 1934. Enthusiasts acclaimed Walter Lindrum's great break of 4,137 in 1932 which took him 175 minutes. A year later he achieved 529 'nursery' or 'clock' cannons. Joe Davis was the Snooker Champion from 1927-39 and beyond, and it was in 1928 that he made his first 100-break at snooker. The great billiard games were played in a building in Leicester Square, the lights shining on the tables, the spectators sitting in shadow round the room, breathless with anticipation.

The magic of Wimbledon was evident. It produced great players and personalities such as Tilden who won the Men's Singles in 1920, 1921 and 1930. Borotra and Lacoste won in 1924 and 1925 respectively and Fred Perry had a clear run in 1934, 1935, and 1936. Suzanne Lenglen, dynamic and temperamental, won the Women's Singles from 1919-23 and in 1925. Helen Wills won in 1927, 1928 and 1929 and as Mrs Moody in 1930, 1932, 1933, 1935 and 1938.

Suzanne Lenglen needed freedom of move-

ment for her energetic game. The conventional clothes in which women played were constricting, and so she discarded her suspender-belt, keeping up her stockings with garters above the knee. Instead of a petticoat, she wore a short, pleated skirt, and in place of long sleeves, a short-sleeved vest. Her first appearance at Wimbledon so attired was the subject of much adverse comment, but her example was followed by others. Lesser lights in tennis clubs up and down the country sported the Lenglen bandeau she wore round her head, and when Helen Wills in 1924 appeared on the Centre Court wearing a prominent eyeshade, this also became fashionable. The Tennis Club became the centre of social life for children of the upper-middle classes. Fond fathers would have the lawn marked out and a net erected, while ambitious mothers mixed cool drinks for eligibly healthy young men.

Recollections of horse racing centre on pictures of the rotund Aga Khan leading in the winner. His horses won the Derby in 1930 (Blenheim) 1935 (Bahram) and 1936 (Mahmoud). Steve Donoghue—with six Derby winners to his credit—was Champion Jockey from 1918 to 1923 when he shared the honour with E. C. Elliott. Elliott was Champion in 1924, and then for the thirteen years after 1925 Gordon Richards was the winner, only missing out to T. Weston in 1926, and F. Fox in 1930.

The Tote was introduced in England in 1928, and legalised by the Racecourse Betting Act of the same year. The Racecourse Betting Control Board kept back part of the proceeds for horse-breeding. The punters' flutter amounted to £230 millions in 1929. The wealthy could place bets on account by telephone; but the man-in-the-street surreptitiously passed betting slips to runners who risked being apprehended by the police.

From horses to dogs. The idea that a greyhound would pay any attention to a dummy hare driven round a track by electricity was ridiculed in some quarters. Dogs were much too intelligent to be taken in by such folly. But the

The Aga Khan leads in his 1930 Derby winner Blenheim with H. Wragg up

Advance. Sandown Park, 1924

Greyhound Racing Association initiated racing in Manchester in July 1926, and this new sport got off, like the greyhounds, to a flying start. If the greyhounds were taken in, then so were the punters. By 1927 there were over sixty greyhound racing companies organising meetings in Scotland, the main provincial cities and at the White City and Wembley Stadium in London. Champion greyhounds such as Max the Miller achieved popularity usually reserved for a Derby winner, or a film star.

The energies of youth found outlets in dirt-track racing in the late twenties. It encouraged the mechanically-minded, created noise, polluted the atmosphere and had the right element of danger that created heroes for worshipping. Both dirt-track and greyhound racing could take place at night under cover, illuminated by arc lamps, and it was in the evenings that the crowds gathered at such events, leaving the daylight hours for football and horse racing.

In the boxing ring it was the day of the hungry fighter. Unemployment in the United States and Britain drove idle youngsters with aptitude to the boxing booths and the gymnasiums. Those with the necessary stamina made good, but the going was hard. The National Sporting Club, founded by John Fleming and A. F. 'Peggy' Bettinson in 1891, did much to encourage the tradition of sportsmanship in boxing. Lord Lonsdale was the first president. Standards were high, and star-studded bouts were staged at the Covent Garden premises. In 1920 the club realised that good boxers could command more money than the seating capacity at the Covent Garden premises could ensure. But after various expedients (which included a move to the Stadium Club in Holborn), the outbreak of war in 1939 delivered the knock-out blow to the NSC as it was originally founded.

In July 1919 Jack Dempsey knocked out the great Jess Willard in the third round to become

Retreat. Ascot, 1935

World Heavyweight Champion, and he defended his title against Billy Miske, Bill Brennan, Georges Carpentier and Luis Firpo until he was deposed by Gene Tunney on points in September 1926. The Dempsey versus Carpentier contest in 1921 was an event of world-wide interest. Carpentier was popular in Europe, and there was a David and Goliath element about this world title fight. It was in the days before simultaneous communication, and it was arranged that an aircraft should fly over Paris and London with green lights if Carpentier won, and with red if it was Dempsey. The contest was over in four rounds and the

ONE GOOD TURN DESERVES ANOTHER

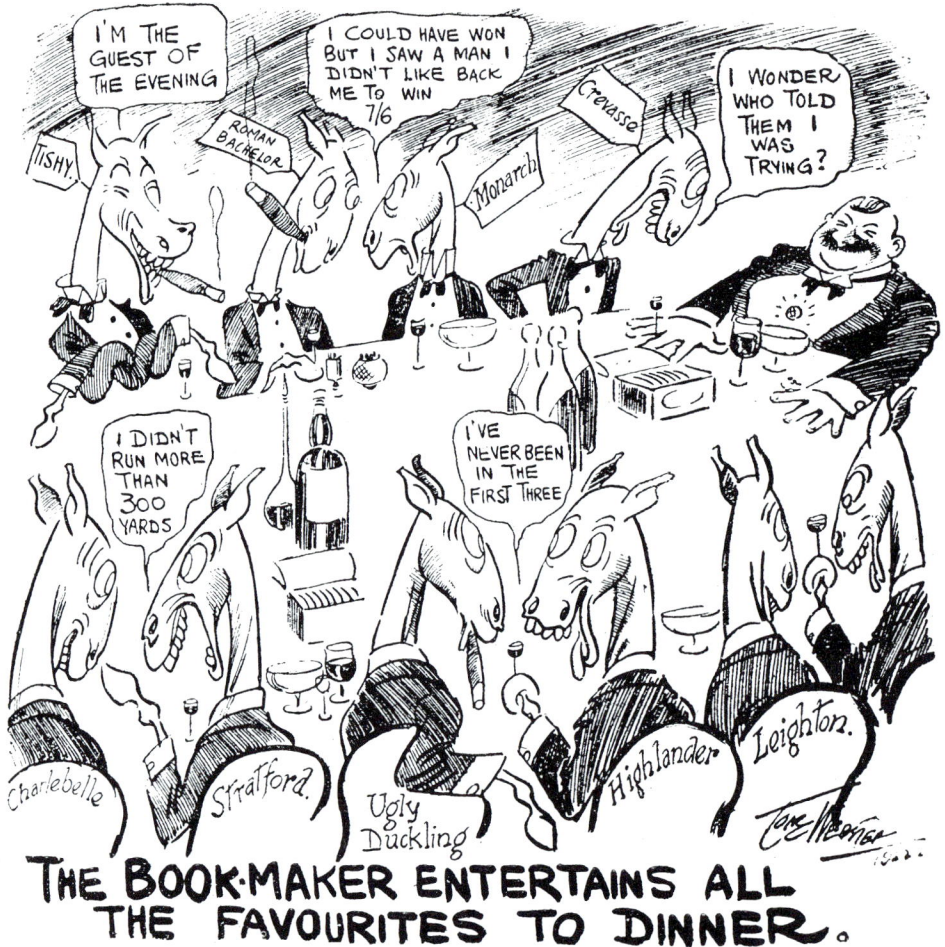

THE BOOK-MAKER ENTERTAINS ALL THE FAVOURITES TO DINNER.

Tom Webster was one of the greatest sports cartoonists of the 1920s and 1930s. Here the bookmaker entertains the racehorses who have persistently lost thereby enabling him to live in the manner in which he is accustomed. Tishy, the horse that was alleged to have crossed its legs during a race was as well known—thanks to Tom Webster— as the most illustrious winner. His cartoons appeared in the Daily Mail

(*above*) *In 1926 there was greyhound racing at Belle Vue, Manchester. Competitors with their handlers before a race.* (*below*) *Dempsey v Carpentier, July 1921. The first million-dollar gate. The place New Jersey, USA. The view of the stadium, a sea of straw hats, the boxers mere specks in the middle distance. Dempsey won and aircraft, with red lights, flew over Europe and engulfed Paris in gloom*

aircraft, its red lights shining, engulfed Paris in such despair that the shops closed. In Britain, too, there was sorrow. Carpentier was handsome and a fine boxer and his lightning disposal of Joe Beckett in 73 seconds in 1919 was still remembered.

Joe Beckett won the British Heavyweight Championship from Billy Wells in February 1919. Throughout the years between the wars the British heavyweight champions lacked the qualities to be world champions. Phil Scott, champion in 1926, lacked the 'killer' instinct; as did Reggie Meen, champion in 1931. Jack Petersen had the courage, but lost his title to Len Harvey in 1933. Tommy Farr took Joe Louis to fifteen rounds in New York's Yankee Stadium in 1937, and outpointed Max Baer the same year, who had been world champion in 1934.

In the World Heavyweight Champion stakes Dempsey gave way to Gene Tunney who retained the title in a return bout and retired unbeaten in 1926. Primo Carnera, winner in 1933, was a giant Italian—known affectionately as the Ambling Alp—standing 6ft 6in in his socks and weighing not far short of 19 stone. A veritable mountain of a man, with more boxing ability than he was credited with. Max Baer toppled him in the eleventh round in 1934, taking the championship from him. James Braddock took the title from Baer in 1935, and in 1937 Joe Louis—the greatest of them all—took the title from Braddock. Louis' reign lasted from 1937 until he retired in 1949, having defended his title twenty-five times.

And in calmer waters, Gertrude Ederle of New York swam the English Channel in 1926. She was the first woman to do so.

Teddy Tail, the 'Daily Mail' and 'write to "John Bull" About it!'

BROADCASTING HAD little effect on the sale of newspapers or the influence of the press. Advertising revenue was not affected, the only other competitors in that sphere being posters on hoardings and direct mail advertising. *The Times, Daily Telegraph* and *Morning Post* were the 'heavies'. Of the three, *The Times* was the accepted voice of Britain, considered by governments overseas to reflect the views of the political party in power. Its front page was filled with classified advertisements including the famous Hatches, Matches and Despatches. In the Personal Column the commercial entries were separated by a rule from those inserted by private individuals, rather as the cricketing

Teddy Tail of the Daily Mail. *If you read the* Daily Mirror Pip, Squeak and Wilfred *were your favourites, and you became a member of the Gugnunc Club*

104

Gentlemen were separated from the Players. It was stuffy in appearance and layout and with a tendency to report sport indulged in by well-bred horses or equally well-bred individuals. It covered political news internationally and devoted some space to books, theatre-going and women's fashions. Its presentations of the news was conservative with seemingly little comprehension of how the other half lived. Politically to the Right, it would bend over backwards to be fair to political parties of which it did not approve, without hiding its obvious distaste for the task. In the 1930s *The Times* considered that the Treaty of Versailles was unjust and that it was wrong to be beastly to the Germans. Its influence was such that when, in a leader, it was suggested that the Sudeten German districts should be ceded to Germany by Czechoslovakia, our future enemies and allies considered such views must have been 'inspired' by the British Government. Most European countries had a 'controlled' press.

In 1922 the circulation of *The Times* was over 200,000 and it cost 1½d. In 1937 the circulation was over 190,000 and the price had risen to 2d. It was edited by Geoffrey Dawson from 1912 until 1941 except for a break between 1919 and 1923.

The *Morning Post* was brilliantly edited, witty, reactionary, upholding the privileges of the upper classes against the dangers from the Left and staunch in its support of King and Country. During the 1914–18 war the price had been increased to 2d but in 1926 it was reduced to 1d. The reduction failed to increase circulation enough to attract the necessary advertising. Fighting a losing battle, it failed to make headway, and on 30 September 1937, with a circulation of 100,000, it merged with the *Daily Telegraph*. The final issue of the *Morning Post* explained to its readers in words which have by now a familiar ring: 'The high costs of production which a London daily newspaper must face today—costs which are shortly to be magnified by a steep rise in the cost of newsprint and by other causes . . . militate heavily against an organ whose appeal is necessarily a limited one.' It was edited by H. A. Gwynne from 1911 until its closure.

The *Daily Telegraph* was read by those who found *The Times* too heavy. Whereas *The Times* was concerned with certainties, the *Daily Telegraph* would chance an intelligent hunch. Unlike *The Times* it would daringly extend a headline across more than a single column. It had at its disposal an impressive number of correspondents, experts in particular fields, and it published pictures. At the end of December 1930, when the price was reduced from 2d to

The Children's Newspaper first appeared in 1919 under the editorship of Arthur Mee. Topics of the day were presented to children sensibly and unsensationally. It ceased publication in 1965 when its 'good taste' was no longer fashionable, and other more blatant forms of communication were available

1d the circulation increased from 100,000 to 215,000 in four months. Nearly six years later half a million was reached. It resisted the temptation to lower standards with the price, its thirty-two pages for 1d providing astounding value. The managing editor during most of the inter-war period and beyond was Arthur E. Watson. The owner and editor-in-chief was Lord Camrose, who acquired the paper in 1927.

So much for the upper hierarchy. The readers were articulate, educated, monied by comparison with the rest of the population and reasonably smug in their security. But there was no newspaper that catered for the world of the vast majority. That was until Lord Northcliffe (as he was to become) took steps to remedy the situation. The *Daily Mail's* first issue was on 4 May 1896. It was a 'penny newspaper that sold for a halfpenny' and it did sell—a record 397,215 copies. Under the guidance of Northcliffe, the *Daily Mail* became phenomenally successful.

Its appeal in its early days was to those who would like to be earning £1,000 a year but were not. The behaviour of the wealthy, topical articles, features for women on clothes, cooking, children, the home—everything in fact around which life revolved or the reader would like it to revolve—were the ingredients. People were of outstanding interest to other people, and the emphasis was on people in relation to what was happening in the world. News must be exclusive if possible, but its presentation—exclusive or not—was of paramount importance. The errand boy, the mill worker, the bank clerk must have their attention gripped. The news in the *Daily Mail* must be a topic of conversation and discussion in the pubs and cafés. All this was far removed from the more rarified atmosphere created by the 'heavies'.

When Northcliffe died in 1922 a revolution in newspaper economics and presentation had taken place. His successor, his brother, the future Lord Rothermere inherited the newspaper which had a daily sale of 1,784,313. Rothermere lacked his brother's popular touch. He championed some unpopular causes and

showed a marked inclination in the 1930s towards Fascism with anti-Jewish undertones. What he lacked in journalistic flair was compensated by his considerable financial abilities.

The *Daily Mail's* chief competitor was the *Daily Express* which was controlled by Lord Beaverbrook after the Great War. In 1920 the *Express* was selling 517,465 copies daily, rising to 793,318 in 1922 when Northcliffe died. Thereafter followed a circulation battle. In 1936 the *Daily Express* reached 2,091,239 in daily sales. Just before World War II, it had reached 2,543,374 to the *Daily Mail's* 1,525,939.

The journalistic approach of the *Daily Mail* during the inter-war years influenced its competitors. The *Daily Herald*, taken over by the Labour Party in 1923 failed until its acquisition by Odhams in 1929 under whose control the Labour Party retained financial interest. In 1939 the *Daily Herald* was selling something over 2 million copies daily. The *Daily Chronicle*, despite the circulation of nearly a million, amalgamated with the *Daily News* in 1930 to become the *Daily News and Chronicle* and ultimately the *News-Chronicle*. There were the pictorial dailies, the *Daily Mirror* and the *Daily Sketch*, each with circulations around the million mark.

Northcliffe had started something which culminated in a ruthless circulation battle, for without circulation, advertising fell away. The *Daily Mail* could command £1,400 for a front page advertisement. It was essential not only to hold on to readers, but to win new ones. The methods employed were varied. Free insurance was available against almost every danger and ill that might beset a human being. The heirs of a married couple killed in a rail accident might receive £10,000 if they read the right paper. Such insurance schemes cost the *Daily Mail* a million pounds, over and above the normal production costs. Other newspapers, compelled to join the battle might have suffered less financially, but it was an intolerable burden. And there was to be no let-up.

The next move was the employment of canvassers—numbering some 50,000—who knocked at the doors of homes up and down the country with sales patter about the advantages of subscribing to a particular newspaper in return for free insurance and a cornucopia of prize money to be won by entering inane competitions. Then followed 'free' gifts of a wide variety from fountain pens to kitchen equipment. Payment? Become a registered reader for ten weeks. It cost the *Daily Herald* £1 per registered reader enrolled this way. The paper cost 1d. The only advantage of the scheme was that the canvassers came from the vast pool of unemployed created by economy drives. They were only too willing to take on the job for £3 a week.

The situation had reached alarming proportions and the Newspaper Proprietors' Association forbade free gifts and ruled that nothing should be offered to readers below cost price. Canvassing was permitted to continue. This edict harmed the *Daily Herald*, the circulation of which was much less secure than the established *Daily Express* and *Daily Mail*. The *Daily Herald* thought up another plan. It offered books to registered readers not below cost but below their real value. This was made possible by cheaper book production methods. Consequently, there appeared complete sets of Dickens, titles such as 'Home Doctor' and 'Handyman', dictionaries—anything to furnish the front room with a bit of culture even though the actual books might never be read. The other newspapers protested but to no avail, so the *Daily Express*, the *Daily Mail* and the *News-Chronicle* issued *their* editions of the classics. In the battles that followed, the circulation of the different newspapers rose and fell according to the offers made. Kitchens had been equipped, pockets had been lined with pens and pencils, next bookcases were stuffed with literature. It all did wonders for the circulation of the *Daily Herald*, but now that the public owned a book—more than one even—the *Herald* was unable to consolidate its circulation gains. It was losing £10,000 a week at one time. The real 1939 war put a stop to such nonsense. Canvassing was no longer

A shot in the circulation battle of the 1930s

possible, newspapers were restricted in size, and after all, there was nothing like a real war to stimulate interest in news. The *Daily Mail* and the *Daily Express* held the field.

It was the day of the powerful newspaper proprietor. Astor (*The Times*), Beaverbrook (the *Express* group), Elias, later Lord Southwood (*Daily Herald*), Rothermere (*Daily Mail*) and others. They were the Press Barons, or Wicked Barons, as their opponents liked to think of them. Some were born into great newspaper families; others had newspapers thrust upon them. In the cut-throat atmosphere of Fleet Street, they had to be ruthless or go under. Their politics and views were reflected in the newspapers they controlled. They were wealthy, and despite their aggressive characters they could—if it was to their advantage—turn on the charm. The battle for circulation was not, in retrospect, an edifying spectacle. And scurrying to do the Barons' bidding were a multitude of editors and journalists in favour at the beginning of a week but with the likelihood of being out on their ear by the weekend.

In 1938 there was launched a magazine called *Picture Post*. Its proprietor was Edward Hulton whose family had been newspaper proprietors, and its editor was Stefan Lorant, a Hungarian refugee who had been imprisoned in Munich by the Nazis. It set out to deal pictorially with the issues of the day. The content of *Picture Post* was a talking point for thousands of young people anxious for information on what was going on in the world. It brought home to people, without fear or favour, what they knew was happening but preferred not to accept. In *Picture Post* there was photographic evidence of the highest order; the accompanying text was a brilliant complement to the visual. There, for all to see, were the horrors, miseries and the happiness surrounding people in Britain, on the continent of Europe and in distant parts, where so many British would be spending a critical period of their young lives. *Picture Post* died in 1950 due partly to television, but more to changes of editorial policy decreed by management. The result was a lowering of standards. The sensational and the trival were no substitute for the integrity for which the magazine was originally acclaimed.

Integrity was not one of the attributes of Horatio Bottomley. Born in 1860 of humble origin and educated, he maintained, at the 'University of Life'. He had two natural gifts—oratory and brashness. Not for him timidity and a retiring nature. His way of life was to think big and never to undersell himself. He swindled the poor with his eloquence, and fooled the rich with his persuasiveness.

His first job in the latter part of the nine-

Horatio Bottomley, top hatted and with the law at his side, leaves Bow Street in 1921

State Express CIGARETTES
555
Number — Virginia
For Discriminating Smokers.

The ★ Star

630

No. 10558.   LONDON, WEDNESDAY, FEBRUARY 22, 1922.   ONE PENNY.   **16 PAGES.**

BOTTOMLEY: PUBLIC PROSECUTOR ACTS.

MRS. PEEL AND THE P.O. "DETECTIVE."

KEEN QUESTIONS ABOUT BETS.

"A LITTLE HEAVIER THAN USUAL."
—Mrs. Peel.

TELEPHONE TALK ON "SALE OF SHARES."

CAPTAIN'S DENIAL.

Mr. Bishop, a Post Office "detective," told at Bow-street to-day how he inquired into the allegations of attempting to defraud bookmakers, brought against Captain Owen Peel and Mrs. Peel, the daughter of Sir Robert Jardine.

FASHIONABLY dressed women again thronged the court, Mrs. Peel was wearing a blue cosumte and red hat as before, and Captain Peel carried a fur-lined coat with him to the seat in front of the dock.

Sir Robert Jardine was among those

MR. BISHOP'S STORY.

Long List of Questions for Mrs. Peel.

Mr. Arthur Henry Bishop, a clerk in the secretary's office at the General Post Office, was the first witness.

He said he received instructions to make inquiries into the case on October 27, and he was handed a number of letters from bookmakers.

A CALL ON MRS. PEEL.

He obtained the original telegrams, and went to Avon Dassett on November 29. He saw Mr. Watts and Miss Cooper, and took statements from them. The same day he called at Avon Carrow to see Captain Peel, who was out. He saw Mrs. Peel.

"I told her I was making inquiries about telegrams sent on October 8," said Mr. Bishop, "and I wished to see Captain Peel.

"She said, 'Captain Peel is not in at present, but I am expecting him. Can I do anything for you?'

"I said 'I will wait until Captain Peel arrives.' I was shown into the smoke-room to wait for him. Sergeant Ambrose, of the Metropolitan Police, attached to the Post Office, was with me."

WAITING FOR THE CAPTAIN.

He waited for some time, and then Mrs. Peel came into the room. She said, "I can't understand Captain Peel being so long. Can I do any

SHADOW OVER THE WEDDING.

Death of Lady Feodora Gleichen.

NO POSTPONEMENT.

A Lord Mayor's Procession to the Palace To-day.

A shadow has been cast upon the preparations for the Royal wedding by the regretted death of Lady Feodora Gleichen at St. James's Palace this morning (reported on page 6).

We are assured, however, that in view of the great public inconvenience that would be caused there will be no postponement of the wedding, and that the Court will not go into mourning for the King's cousin.

PRINCESS MARY and Viscount Lascelles are accompanying the King and Queen on their visit to the Shire Horse Show to-day.

During the morning the Princess and the Viscount received several deputations who brought wedding presents.

The Lord Mayor, Sheriffs, and Aldermen of the City of London went in 16 carriages to present an address and a piece of jewelry.

The civic party all wore their robes of office, and the City Marshal, in full-dress uniform, preceded the Lord Mayor's semi-state carriage on horseback.

A large crowd assembled outside the Palace to witness the arrival of the procession.

The deputation was conducted to the reception room by the officers of

BOTTOMLEY ACCUSED OF CONVERTING FUNDS.

SUMMONS SERVED TO-DAY: TRIP TO PARIS CANCELLED.

BOW-STREET HEARING ON MARCH 8.

SIR ARCHIBALD BODKIN, Director of Public Prosecutions, applied in person to Mr. Chester Jones, the Bow-street magistrate, yesterday, and was granted a summons against Mr. Horatio Bottomley, M.P.

The application was made privately. Mr. Bottomley read the news to-day, and rang up Scotland Yard to inform the authorities that—

He had intended to go to Paris this week on business, but in view of the statement in the press that the Public Prosecutor was issuing a summons against him, he had cancelled the journey.

CHARGE OF CONVERSION.

The summons was served on him at 12.50 this afternoon.

He is charged with converting to his own use £5,000, part of the property of the Victory Bond Club, on September 16, 1919.

The summons is returnable for March 8. The case will be heard at Bow-street.

It was stated in a morning paper that "this is a speedy sequel to Mr. Bottomley's challenge to the Director of Public Prosecutions, following upon the acquittal of Mr. Reuben Bigland at Shrewsbury."

This is not strictly true. The so-called "challenge" was only issued to the press on Monday, and the Public Prosecutor is neither so simple nor so quick in action as to accommodate Mr. Bottomley with proceedings on lines of his own choosing.

NOT A SEQUEL TO CHALLENGE.

It will be found that the action of the authorities has been taken after long and most careful consideration. It could not have been taken while the Bigland case was still sub judice, and that it is taken now makes it, perhaps, a "sequel" to the Bigland verdict, but certainly not a sequel to Mr. Bottomley's challenge.

Horatio Bottomley's last move

---

teenth century was with a firm of solicitors. There he saw for himself the rewards of the rich, especially the rich who had obtained money fraudulently. After a spell as a Police Court writer, he came to the conclusion that although honesty might well be the best policy, it was the least rewarding one.

At twenty-six years of age, he became a chairman of a publishing company. This was a mere stepping stone to acquiring a financial empire which he conducted with an air of mystery from the luxury suites of foreign hotels. Little, if any, business was done. The shareholders' suspicions were better founded than the business, which appeared to exist only in name. Bottomley was made bankrupt. He wrote a letter to the accountants who had dealt with his bankruptcy thanking them for their assistance and ending, 'I shall certainly advise all my friends as they become bankrupt, to avail themselves of your services.'

His misfortunes created publicity. His flamboyance and oratory cast a spell over his listeners and those he needed to impress. Australian gold mines, finance corporations in London—he launched anything for which he could get money. People poured it into his lap and seemed strangely prepared to accept his silver-tongued explanations when dividends failed to materialise.

His influence in Fleet Street was considerable. He founded the *Financial Times*, owning other papers for a period, and launched the successful *John Bull* which he edited and which formed a platform for his views and outspoken opinions. Here, thought his millions of readers, was a man of the people. He was elected to parliament as a Liberal from 1906 to 1912 and again from 1918 until 1922, although the leaders of the party had the gravest suspicions about him. Racehorses, mistresses, kippers and champagne for breakfast—a man larger than life whose possessions and antics seemed to hypnotise those who led honest but dreary existences. He stood in Trafalgar Square and appealed for recruits to fight the Hun. He visited troops in France and accepted with a show of diffidence a generous sum of money from the British Government for his morale-building efforts.

His War Savings Certificates, which became the Victory Bond club in 1918, appealed to people's patriotism and seemingly gave the most humble citizen the opportunity to get rich. Each Victory Bond sold at £1 each. Numbered discs were placed in a sack and drawn out, in an atmosphere of secrecy, by Bottomley himself. The lucky numbers—nearly 2,000 of them—were published in the press, but who *were* the winners? No names and addresses were published and finally it became clear that the real and sole winner was Horatio Bottomley. When accused he was most indignant, but to no avail and he was charged with fraud in May, 1922. In court he played all his talents—eloquence, brashness, emotional outbursts—but it was too late. After an eight-day trial he was sentenced to seven years' penal servitude. He bounded back after his release to start a new weekly, *John Blunt* in 1928. In 1933 he died, but not before he had toured the halls pathetically relating incidents from his 'scandalous past'. The magic had gone.

Bottomley was at the height of his powers before and during World War I, but his energy and eloquence carried him forward to the inter-war years. He was an example of that period, not so much by nature of his crimes, but by the figure he presented to the public. Here was a self-made, self-educated man; a free spender in the wine, women and song tradition. His behaviour could always catch the headlines of the popular press which at that time was doing so much to falsify values. He was indeed a fit subject for the inter-war years.

ACKNOWLEDGEMENTS

To Mr John Frost of the Historical Newspaper Service; to the Music Room of the British Museum; to the Enthoven Collection, Victoria & Albert Museum; to Messrs Arthur Guinness for permission to quote the verse on page 64; to Mr H. E. Bray and his staff of the Illustrated London News and Sketch Syndication Department.

Also to the authors and publishers of books too numerous to mention, but in particular to *Between the Wars 1918–1940* by C. L. Mowat (Methuen, 1955) and *The Long Weekend* by Robert Graves and Alan Hodge (Faber, 1950).

Illustrations are acknowledged below. Much inter-war photographic material was either destroyed by enemy action, or jettisoned. Although every effort has been made to trace the copyright owners, this has not always been successful.

Ashmolean Museum, 73; Associated Newspapers Group Ltd, 7 (bottom), 23, 102, 104, 109; Barnaby's Picture Library, 28 (both); The Birmingham Post & Mail Ltd, 65; British Overseas Airways Corporation, 94, 95; Cassell & Co Ltd, 37; Central Press Photos Ltd, 9, 15, 16 (both), 17, 18 (top), 22, 29, 53 (top), 108; Colorsport, 98 (top); Conway Picture Library, 41; *Daily Express*, 19; *Daily Telegraph*, 33 (top); EMI-Pathe Film Library, 6, 7 (top), 8 (both), 25, 26, 31 (both), 33 (bottom), 34, 47 (bottom), 49 (bottom), 57, 58 (all), 74 (bottom), 75, 93 (all), 96, 97 (top), 99; Fortnum & Mason Ltd, 70 (bottom); H. Heynes & Co, Eastbourne, 30; Kodak Museum, 'The Kodak Girl' by Fred Pegram, 68; London Transport, 91; David Low cartoon on page 18 by arrangement with the Trustees and the *Evening Standard*; Angus McBean photograph, Harvard Theatre Collection, 80; Raymond Mander and Joe Mitchenson Theatre Collection, 84; National Film Archive, 53 (bottom), 54 (all), 55, 56 (both); *The Observer*, 35; Peter Maurice Music Co, 61; Popperfoto, 27; Press Association Ltd, 38 (both), 40, 52; *Punch*, 44, 46, 67, 72, 87, 89; Radio Times Hulton Picture Library, frontispiece (both), 11 (all), 12, 42, 48, 49 (top), 50 (bottom), 60 (left), 63, 68 (right), 92, 98 (bottom), 100, 101 (both), 103 (both); Reckitt & Colman, 70 (top); W. H. Smith & Son Ltd, 36; Mrs Joyce Stone, 50 (top); *Sunday Express*, 43; Syndication International Ltd, 105, 107; Yevonde, 78 (right); Song sheets, pages 76, 85, 86: Lawrence Wright Music Company Ltd, 'On the Sunny Side of the Street' © 1930, 'Ain't She Sweet?' © 1927, 'C-o-n-s-t-a-n-t-i-n-o-p-l-e' © 1928; Herman Darewski Music Publishing Co Ltd, 'Ours is a Nice House Ours Is'; B. Feldman & Co Ltd, 'I'm Forever Blowing Bubbles'; Francis, Day & Hunter Ltd, 'It Ain't Gonna Rain No Mo' '; Chappell & Co Ltd, 'You Are My Heart's Delight', 'Little Man You've Had a Busy Day'; Campbell Connelly & Co Ltd, 'Ain't it Grand to be Blooming Well Dead'; Victoria Music Publishing Co Ltd, 'Thanks for the Memory'.

INDEX